MW01224453

2nd edition 2013

...poems and prose of unbridled optimism
for the tent bound

\*\*\*\*\*\*\*\*\*\*

Published by
Habayim Publishing
Victoria, BC Copyright © 2002
Web Online Publication © 2013
All Rights Reserved

jaysrs1@yahoo.ca

# Contents

## About the Author

Jay Danis is a man of the high north, the mountains and peaks, the rivers and the timberline. An incurable romantic, his poetry is a mixture of 'cracker barrel humor' and far-fetched tales of tragedy in the high north. In the style of Robert Service he takes us back to an era of simplicity, of honor and valor, of the rapscallion saloon dwellers, honorable thieves and rogues. Playing no small role in these folk tales are the ever present men of the North West Mounted Police, the predecessor of the Royal Canadian Mounted Police. There are noted clashes between fleeing criminals and Mounties who doggedly pursue to 'always get their man'. The character of Constable McCue is real, though the author admits the piece entitled 'McCue of the Mounted' is an extreme stretching of the truth. This poem was inspired by the painting by C. Caldwell, 'Hero in Red Serge'. Mike Doyle still concocts his mayonnaise and the author distances himself from the process whenever Mike is brewing his famed cure all. Yukon Kenny is out there somewhere and was known to have still been alive in 1997. The tale of the 'Moose Cakes' is based on fact for the most part.

Born in southern Ontario Jay first heard 'the call of the north' he recalls, while laying awake in his uncle's home tucked deep in the north woods of Algonquin Park in 1959. Always a woodsman: even in his formative years, like his father he never betrayed that calling. He served in the RCAF and found himself on the Pinetree Radar Line of the north. Ideally he pursued these tales in remote bars and small hamlets there, deliberately seeking out the characters who formed the basis of his poetry and stories. Eventually he became a Law Enforcement Consultant: almost exclusively to the RCMP while at the same time serving as crew chief of an elite 'high angle rope rescue team' with Search and Rescue BC. Jay now lives in semi-retirement in Edmonton, Alberta.

It is the author's sincere desire that this collection of his poetry leaves its' readers warm of heart and fulfilled.

Dedication

To those who have ever been tent bound by weather and those who inspired me...

...my Mother, retired RCMP Constable Wally McCue, Doug Yearwood, Mike Doyle, Frank Santo, Will Sherman, Mark Meincke, Scottie Cole the bush pilot, Rob Chisnall, Mac MacCormack with whom I shared so many boyhood adventures on the Nith River and all the others who have encouraged and brought out the...imp in me.

Thank you.

Authors' Note...

For the most part punctuation is absent in these pieces so as to allow the reader to set their own rhythm and pace.

## Strongquill of the Mounted

Strongquill of the Mounted was a veteran of
dangerous pursuit
Cross Canada's hills and plains he went proud in the
scarlet-coated suit
Those of blackened heart tread light, the time sticks
are burning and lit
Run if they may, they'd not get away
For Strongquill never quit

He'd given his vow and sworn an oath
 "Maintiens Le Droit" till the end
Thus he did on that snowy day
 When God's own troop was sent

"The Marines are away right now," said the Lord
"Who'll guard heaven's gates I fear?"
So Michael the Pillar of angels spoke out
 "There's a choice but one for us here"

So Strongquill the Mountie was called away
Where only angels have trod
He's gone to man a special post...
To stand guard at the throne of God


*Dedicated to Constable Dennis Strongquill*
*Royal Canadian Mounted Police*
*Died at his post December 2001*

## The Righteous Four

Snow patches graced the Mother Earth's face
In the cold, crisp chill of the night
The stars like beacons hung in the sky
Sparkling above "The Righteous Four's" eyes.
A valorous band these mounted ones
Standing their post at need.
Four of our best on the plains of the west
These men of the RCMP.

But evil knows no season
No right, no purpose, no reason
Justice denied a madman crept by
Silently lurking he skulked

When the pale dawn broke o'er the prairie hills
As if a shroud was laid
An omen of tragedy yet to befall
Those who had risen to duty's call

You may dwell on the evil if you wish or...
Stand in the light the brave have spread
Shed your tears then...
Raise your head
Had "The Great Spirit" run short of shades?
A wonder!
Could nature's easel run dry?
At days end came sunset
The land blazed with scarlet...
As "The Four" rode off cross the skies

## Kalu

Of all the dogs of the north I knew
There was none quite like the one named Kalu.
No full growed husky thought himself such a pup
Quite like he did when he rolled and jumped up

Once he'd decided to do whatever he'd do
He'd do that whatever at a whim
He'd somersault through drifts of snow
He'd draw you beside him and not let go

Now Frank and me worked the station house nights
To flag the trains, sort the mail and tell lies
At times when the telegraph acted a dunce
His master came in to tinker the wires
And at his side along for the ride
Was Kalu our mascot insisting

Don't leave him at home for he won't stay alone
You might as well bring him along
He was owned by a friend and loved by all
And once you were picked that was it
You'd love him and spoil him
With no shame to your soul
For the fella would simply not let you go

I'll admit though I'm damned we spoiled him awful
With treats aplenty and bowls of fresh water
I've wondered often and I think it most certain
He thought Frank and me his kin

# Tales of the High North

Now I've seen some odd sights on cold freezing
nights
At the feet of the midnight sun
Then one cold night in the flickering lights
 I glanced up from my letters stunned
And there as before so often he did
Sat Kalu the insistent husky dog kid

His master was absent and the pup was a'bent
He'd slipped his tether and run off
Straight to our shack with the privy out back
He shamelessly pawed the frost crusted step
Lo' he'd run off for a midnight snack

So later that night in the pale false dawn
His master gazed with brow upraised
Kalu lay curled by the pot bellied stove
Contented and dreaming of days on the rove
Of his kingdom and subjects the deer and the wolf

I often times ponder the chaos he makes
In the land where pets go when the heavens bell tolls
Free of all earthly bonds, on the day of their great
wakin up
And if the devil don't catch me
 I'll slip heavens gate expecting
…to see that old lively husky pup

## Bear Leg

I'd set out on the trail with my winter furs
A poke of dust in my pack
The mid day sun was tanning my face
And the spring breeze at my back

I was headed down to Fort Liard
For grub stake and needed tools
Provisioning swift I'd turn around
According to my own rules

The only love ever faithful I'd had was high in the
passes white
Where nature constant, exotic gives all one needs for
life
The nuggets had fairly jumped in the sleuce
And sang of a banner year
Larder laid up in the pantry
Contented, with no need to fear

I saw the elk and moose
The otter and beaver too
As I tramped along the river gulch
Until about nigh noon

I lit a fire and burned some beans
Coffee perked nice and strong.
I tossed the crumbs of sourdough
For chipmunks what happened along

Carefree or careless I never really knew
But the smell of grub a cooking

Was a scent that stewed and grew
Attractin the wild from far and wide
...the 'Northern Jays' swooped and flew

Back out on the trail again
My God it sure was good.
Until that hairy, frothing beast
Came out of the aspen wood

Circlin bout the fire ring pawin the gravel and
throwing his head
A fight was in the offing lad and one would end up
dead
The grizzly that rose was nine foot tall, a ton of
muscle and maw
Yellow eyed and ready to eat the creature that he saw

So I reached for my trusty old rifle
I stood and drew a bead
Misfire! Damn I'm doomed
But a moiler's a hardy breed

I grabbed my knife and hatchet determined to go
down hard
He rushed and clamped his jaw like a trap around my
lower part
My leg inside his mouth he rose and tossed me all
about
The pain was great as any I'd known, it took all I had
to shout
 "If I be goin under 'bar' I'm damned sure takin you
out"

His claws as big as a harvester's scythe
He mauled me like a sapling spruce
I slashed and hacked a deadly blow
His blood shot like a sleuce

The grizz collapsed there on the bank
And I lay cut and sore
I gazed down where my leg had been
But wasn't anymore

I hacked off the grizzly's left leg at the knee
Dried the thing out and attached it to me
Now one leg carries a boot
And the other leg's furry and clawed
I get the strangest looks from kids
And others exclaim, "Oh my god!"

I have to admit it sickened me some
When first I saw that bloodied lump
Now I'm known as 'Bear Leg' far and wide
The man with the grizzly stump

## Sons of the Trackless Forests

I am a son of the trackless lands
Deep in their couch my spirit dwells
Upon the air the piney pine
That urges my heart to leap and swell

I trod the trackless forests dark
T'is fresh and clean as the mountains streams
Where every creature is free to live
To roam, to pass, to love and dream

The air so sweet where the moss like mesh
Hangs from the towering pines
Where the cougar and grizzly in solitude live
Neath giant spruce and darkening lines

In the early morn when daily is born
A world ever changing unseen
My spirit lifts to the scent of the glade
Where the lark casts its song through the trees

Nature's caresses, banish all cares and stresses
In a place where her laws never change
Where harmony is certain I see and I sense
Though I covet I confess to pass through its sacred
range

And who can tell in the lanes of the dell
The scent of the moon in the light before dawn
The virgin floor of moss, of fallen leaf and limb
The sons of the trackless forests
…go ever on and on

## Song of the Winds

It's heard on the plains and high on the peaks
And the song the wind utters is one that bespeaks
O'er grasslands and valleys it sings through the pines
It sets and orders the passage of time

Its gusts give off so eerily as they conjure its
whispered tune.
By the cry of the night hawk, the morning dove
and the solitary loon
The wind sings its chorus to the wastelands and
mountains an insistent infinite croon

Mournful at times a chill to the soul
Sometimes joyous it makes the heart whole
Lifting mans spirit up high in the clouds
Adrift on the air through billowing shrouds

Inimitable notes from a harp unseen
It foretells of the changes and seasons
As if from the very first day
Before life sprang on that day
All ordered to Gods own reasons

The blue northers howl like a wolf pack at prowl
And oft times chill the brave to the bone
A demon, a fiend to one all alone
Crying out for a mercy and longing for home

Through the treeline pines where the ravens call
And the eagle rides on its drafts
The breeze it seems in a language unknown

Conjures the snow demons laugh

And later sings softly through green aspen leaves
When spring is on the rise
When the care ridden moilers head out on the trail
Lifting their weary eyes

## The Red Coat Trail

T'was their righteous quest to bring law to the west
In the wild and untamed days
Of whiskey traders and scoundrels alike
To prod them south by day and night
By fist and boot or lancers pike
For lack of all their goods they'd sold
A once proud nation of people laid low
Their livelihood taken
Left out in the cold

Miles and miles a rump bustin ride of black fly, forest
and plains
Of burning sun and swollen gorge and damn the
bursting rains
T'was by their deeds a legend was born ever true to
their code
Determined the Red Coats surged, mounted, marched
and rode

The hooch horde heard in 'Whoop Up' fort
The news just was not good…

The North West Mounted advancing.
Sabers drawn and horses a prancing
Pressing on, press ever on, relentless to their goal
The west would be claimed the west would be tamed.
For the right t'is for he who is bold

The wagons and mules all tethered
The lawless made their break
South in a line like a crow flies

Dazed and wailing in their wake

A slinking band of ne'r do goods
A swarm of lice ridden vermin
Curs each one see how they run
As if on winged feet
Raising the dust oh how they cussed
Polecats in retreat

So thus the trail was blazed
Upon the prairie lands
The legend now recounted
Of the gallant Red Coat band

## Bush Trains of the North

A lonesome echo resounding across the forest hills
Bestirs an eerie presence
The engine and whistle afar
That sweeps the night in a formless wave
Beneath heavens mantle of stars

The loon upon the northern lakes
And through the shadowed pines
Knows well the haunting clarion call
Of the bush trains in the night

It soothes the forest creatures
In a mourning voice soft and clear
That all is well in the lands far beyond
The havens of moose the otter and deer

The trapper knows well only he can tell
How the distance melts in the darkness
O'er the miles far away till break of day
With the ring of the engines bell

Sleep, sleep close your eyes in peace
The land about you is calm
So be still, so still, dream the dream of the ageless
And await the golden dawn

## Feeding the Bears
*...Fast Food on the Foot*

There once was a trapper I knew
Who'd killed him more than his due
Many the scars he bore
For the animal skins he wore

Ha ha, he thought a scheme I'll wrot
with the scent glands of a deer
Cunning I am I'll lure the bears near
and black powder ball will take them

So he climbed a tree in ambush
And black bear he killed by the score
Thought himself a wizard
In the presence of his gore

At end of day he wandered away
The deer scent on his boots forgotten
The path of a grizzly sow he crossed
Unknowing of what he'd begotten

Now the grizz hadn't eaten for many a day
The trapper carelessly sloughing
Unaware of the ghastly fate he'd framed
Whistling, striding and loping

Like a slave to her nose the bruin strained
And straight for him she charged...
A ton of angry, hungry bear
Raking him with her claws
Chomping down on his white skinned neck

Trapping him in her jaws

Of a mercy none.
The awful deed was done
The sourdoughs neck was broked…

Be careful where you trod
Tread softly if you do
Fer Griz is always hungry
And seldom sated too
Act the fool in a savage land
You'll see what nature deals
You'll swiftly find return in kind
And end up a bruins meal

footnote: (In the North you're fast or you're fast food)

## The Frost King

You can hear his white wolf myrmadons
On a night when the hoar frost falls.
When the air cracks and snaps from his freezing
breath
Where the demons of hades call

He is the King of the frostlands
Seated high upon his throne
He coats the land in a chilling drape
That creeps right through to your bones

From the pole to the arctic circle
And points untold below
When the ice worms dance and the air tis froze
That it hurts to breathe his breath up your tingling
nose

When fresh brewed coffee freezes
Before it reaches yer lips
Toes are froze, yer nose is froze
Fingers all black at the tips

On crisp clear nights neath the northern lights
When the ice devils dance in a frozen scene
And game is unknown and sparse is life
Not a human sign to be seen

The Frost King deals out moilers justice
T'is he who decides your fate
From his throne at the pole a heart of stone
His red eyed pack circling round

Slaves to the scent slaves to their bent
Slaves to their hunger pangs
Drooling and pacing their wolf hearts racing
Gnashing their silvery fangs
Snapping and scrapping to win first taste
Of this moiler adrift on the far flung wastes

## Ice Pilots

There came a trek for an arctic wreck
A plane t'was said went down
The searchers high in a white out sky
Had failed to sight a sign

From his outpost a Mountie trudged
His Inu guide in the lead
They'd not abandon a man on the wastes
For one left to die was against their creed

The steady malamute sniffed the air
For scent of carcass and great white bear
Neath dancing lights cross the arctic skies
From break to break as northward they plied
The wastes were wide and savage
Beaten by arctic gales and ravaged
For nature pares at bare rock and ice
And makes no wager on taking ones life

With the winds savage howls,
The creatures all cower
And the white scapes change
With each passing hour

From Yellowknife braved the Ice pilots bold
Regulations be damned a skyway man
Missing in that freeze broken and cold

Though blinded by night, by day the sky white
The turbulence tossed them about
No sleep or rest in their sky bound nest

Till the spotters gave a shout

He's there below in the top hard snow
A crumpled hulk of metal and rod
A feeble wave from a man in pain
Salvation at last... Oh thank God!

## The Young Turk

When the autumn leaves, lay crisp and coloured
Upon the forest floor
When the dawn like crystal dew approaches
And opens nature's door
When the great buck deer gives it's warning call amid
the woodland echoes
It's time to clean the bore and breach
To ready for the morrow

Above the vale stands the granite rock
Where the buck's tines crash and lock
The men of the woods gather a'for dawn
Impatiently waiting each tick of the clock

'Twas a day such as this the lad begged his Dad
"Take me please, with you on the hunt"
But the others 'twas feared
Saw just a stripling, to them no more than a runt

Now Ronny the guide when he spoke to the Dad these
were the words he said,
"No! absolutely not"
"We need no kids here for the hunt 'tis sure
Is the place of men, the true shots"

This is a place of heart
"They gather and camp to hunt the deer
And a small boy like yours would get in the way
He'll frighten all the game I fear"

But the father persisted and rightly insisted

"Give the lad a chance"
So just after dawn in the new morning's sun
Three cracks of a rifle rang out
Ho! they laughed, "to shoot that fast
Tells of a miss for sure"

But after the hunt when they gathered him up
They asked how with three shots he'd missed?
Well says he, "I know one is there and one by the
riven oak
 I'm not really sure but you might take a look
And find another one there, by the clearwater brook"
"Well look at that!" said the Dad, "I guess he's fooled
me too"
"Never has a young boy fired a rifle, so sure, so
straight, and true"

He is gone from us now, taken too soon
But his spirit is there at the dawn
So when the reddened leaves lay crisp upon the
autumn ground
And the 'Master of Life' spreads his warmth about
encompassing all around
You'll sense him there at the forest door
He lives on the breeze, in our thoughts evermore

*Dedicated to my friend Turk Yearwood*

## Alpenglow

Rock and ice spindrift snow…
Here is my kingdom this is my place
The howling winds, gendarmes and verglace
Conquering my fears, enriching my soul
For I have been where the clouds can go

Dedicated to Conrad Kain  - Canadian Mountaineer

## Elk Rider

Now Ken Munro of Yukon fame
In his youth and prime to the north thus came
Seeking fortune and finding none
He signed on the line and the deed was done
He'd swore his oath to the RCMP
And his wilding days were ended
He'd "Maintiens Le Droit" rid the north of sin
Chase the villains and shackle their limbs

Or so some thought...
No blustery Sergeant or NCO could ever quite rid
him of guile
That rugged demure and twinkling eye
Would always betray his insufferable smile

Because you see…
Mountie Munro loved a joke
There are tales a plenty of strange things done
In the land of the midnight sun
Gruesome deeds of bullet and blood
Neath the bright blue Yukon skies
T'is there such legends and myths abound
And many just outrageous lies

But the tale of the Mountie and the water logged elk
Is a tale no one can deny

They'd ordered him out on the trail to patrol
To the 'Wolverine Cut' by the Crystal Lake shores.
Where the posts canoe was stashed
And his trapper guide awaited

# Tales of the High North

At break of day he was up and away arriving in time
for lunch
Where he spotted an elk swimming calmly along
And the devil inside him took hold
I'm going to do what no one has done I'll do it at a
whim
Strip my red serge jacket off and
Ride an elk on the swim

Launch the canoe, bring my paddles too
Get in and catch up that elk
Their paddles a froth as the craft leapt forth
Gaining with each plunging stroke
Up side the elk they rapidly swept
For Munro would have his joke

He stripped off his tunic and Stetson too
Gave a shout and dove for its back
He grasped at an antler, the wapatee shreaked
Wild eyed, heaving and crazed
The beast swam on as the lake water churned
Our hero bold, soon renowned
He had his prey and he'd not give way
Till the elk's mighty legs touched ground

When the moment came he released his prize
Triumphant in what he'd done
The elk gave forth in a vengeful screech
An omen of what would come
When the Mountie returned with his guide to their
camp
They gazed on Lucifer's haunt

For the place was a mess and all in a wreck
Supplies scattered there about
He wanted to curse he wanted to shout...
He'd only himself to blame
It seemed an awful price to pay
For his legendary fame

...and from a distance across the hills they heard, the
mocking echo of the great bull elk!

*Based on a true story*

## The Truce

The strangest scene I suppose I saw
I was hold up from the storm
In a stinking grotto of half chewed bones
Where some smelly varmit had once made a home

I lit a fire and gazed o'er my shoulder
As the wind howled and whistled outside
And way back far in that musty hole
 I could see the critters peering angry eyes

They were red and firey
His teeth gnashed bright
And I shook like a frightened child
When he slinked into the light

T'was a wolverine and fighting mad
And I was trapped and chilled
But now my blood was up because
One of us... was sure to be killed

He wouldn't give ground and neither would I.
It was either a truce or we'd both surely die
A fiercesome fight I knew he could give
No time to swing my gun and lay sights

Clenching my knife I gave a grin
In the dancing light of the flames
I grunted and grinned and snorted like him
And we neither one moved an inch

We laid up for days

# Tales of the High North

In each others gaze
He chawed on them bones
And I chawed on my chaw
Neither one lapsed or gave ground

At dawn the third day
The gale passed away
I was out and far from that cave
Thanking my maker I'd live to see
My old weathered cabin and sleuce

Call me a liar, I tell you the truth
T'was the skunk bear and me
In an uneasy truce

## The Barrens

The sweep of the Barrens is savage and wild
T'will break your heart as a motherless child
Or lift you up where no man has been
And show you sights that were never seen

Where the howl of a wolf can chill a man's heart
And make one long for home
But the northern lights as they sweep the skies
Will urge you on to roam
The trappers' the one who's trapped
His heart held in a grip
While the wiley fox glides unseen past his camp
He dreams of each winters trip

Warm and snug in his buffalo rug
The night fire sings its song
The crack and snap of distant ice
While the arctic owl hoots far and long

He knows a peace so few might know
In a place they fear among the snows
White through the day and blue in the moon
The southers are empty and die much too soon

The barrens seem cruel to the city bred fool
But oh how a man is free
By choice he may choose the fringe of the pole
Or gaze on the Beaufort Sea

The Barrens are home to the stunted spruce
The wolverine, wolf, the otter and moose

There's larder fill o'er every hill
Oh what fine neighbors these!

So the trapper he's happy barren bound
To sled his way o'er the open ground
To whistle a tune to the husky's yelp
And pity the damned half - soul southers
Trapped in the cities down south

## McCue of the Mounted
*( inspired by the painting 'Hero In Red Serge' by C.Caldwell )*

Now McCue of the Mounted had hunkered down
Neath the mid winter's moon as it peaked
O'er an icy mount at 40 below
Just south of Dawson Creek

He had no choice but take repast
Though the ghostly wolves bid him nigh
His battle scarred malamute, curled at his feet
Keeping watch with it's one good eye

Tomorrow's trail would take them deep
To the Black Ice Valley round
Where t'is said no bearded arctic hair
Nor fox or bird is found

Where death was more familiar
Than sun in the springtime melt
So cold this place upon man's face
That each laboured heartbeat is felt

But duty called him forth
From his Belle at the "Nugget Saloon"
Two weeks now he'd been out on the trail
Neath the milky waning moon

All Dawson mourned, cloaked in dread
For none of the cursed in 'Lucifer's Hearth'...
Where a mans breath froze, and the cold burned like fire

# Tales of the High North

Ever returned undead

The big Swede had begged the Mountie
His heart rending cry all could hear
His bride just new, had wandered off to that dreaded
Valley he feared

Now the Scarlet coated troopers doubtless, were men
of great renown
Guardians of the right t'is said
By their creed each one honor bound

To always get their man, they'd vowed
Through fire, claw and fang
Never to weaken or relent until the villain was
chained

In their manual it is written
And there it can be seen
The means are just as righteous
As all heroic deeds

The half frozen Mountie pressed on
When the pale gloom of morning came
Upon the wind a child 's wail
And a desperate woman's scream

The Trapper, the Sourdough, a 'Dance Hall' girl, her
precious bird as well
He'd found them all who'd disappeared in the depths
of that black iced hell
He cinched them together one and all dragging each
ghost behind

His pack horse defiant, his frost coated mount,
forming a straggling line

When a bad tempered Grizzly decided t'would be
sport to interfere
With a cuff from his left, McCue gave him his best,
as if to warn him fair
"Not now you mangy slew foot
You've a nerve to bother me bear"

The Mountie never returned, some claim he's out
there still
Think you t'is a yarn I've spun?
Then join them....
If you will

## The Ogre

I climbed a mountain ascending to the sky
Where ice and granite do abide
On that great wall of sudden death I lost my life
Her tears are shed for me
My lonely mourning wife
I swing there still on the winds of time
as spring draws nigh
But I am still alive
I'll always be alive
For I will never die...

*Dedicated to Stephano Longhi - Killed on the Eiger*

## Ice Dogs

I spend my nights telling lies to the ladies
Whenever I sled into Franklin Bay
Ah, Franklin now sleeps with the frozen dead
He vanished in the arctic wastes t'is said
So there lays his marker in eerie jest
His shrivelled hand frozen and pointing west

The arctic tundra is home to the graves
Of moilers and toilers who gainst nature's ways
By snowshoe and sled as they sallied forth
Tried to conquer the white frozen north

A waste their élan, their vigour and sweat
For the land always wins in the end
And men in their foolishness end up half crazed
Losing their sleighs and losing their way

Starving and froze, missing half their toes
Whimpering, crying over their mothers left mourning
For sons long lost on the barrens and wastes
Southers just don't have the sand in their veins
Don't have the wits and don't have the grit
To hold to themselves and make a last stand
As the gods who'd create such vast frozen lands

The diggers and damned, the poisoned and maimed
Pay a frightful price for the lands that they've claimed
High in the north in a frozen froth, of stormy gale and
steel breaking cold
'Tis the huskies that jest as they curl in the drift
And the malamutes dance their dance

Snarling and jeering at all the fuss
The dogs eye waiting for the moilers last cuss
The weather is grand except for the damned
He'll make a fine meal when he drops

## The Orendas

Lurking along the forest trails
Or out on the barrens where the blue northers wail
Near water pools and raging chutes
Possessing the wolves and the malamutes
Till an unwary human comes by

They imp or do evil whatever their whim
Light as a sparrow upon the wind
They're the owl in the night, the wisp of a breeze
Feel the cold wary chill of the watched, now flee!

Run fast and far through the bracken and snow
No time to linger for now you must go
From that wee cloud of down cross a hunters moon
A snow devil raising a strange sort of plume

Make haste as you dash with your rifle and cache
Seek out the rill where no one will find you
Bury yourself in goss and frost
Remain ever silent in the land of the lost

Orendas come from the spirit land
Orendas are part of the ghostly band
And if one takes a shine to you
Good fortune or bad is certain
And all in the north say it's true

But a devilish crew may follow you
A gentle touch or a nasty shove
The snap of a trap or soft as a dove
They enter the mind driving moilers insane

And though what's seen may not be clear
They drive men mad with terror and fear...
Pray for salvation Gods angels to keep...
The Orendas at bay while you seek peace in sleep

## Sourdoughin

In the days of the Klondike gold rush
The night air crisp as glass
A diamond topped layer of new fallen snow
Lay fresh in the Big Horn Pass
Malamutes mangy and growlin
Rebuked by man and beast
The arctic wolves out prowlin
With a hunger that never ceased

Free from the bonds of man
Gods lantern shelf agleam
A man half froze, half starved
Battling the struggling team

Rich beyond his greatest dreams
A sled laden down with gold
If only the Post were nearer
He wouldn't fear this cold

Ice worms danced neath the mid winter's moon
In the land of the midnight sun
The sleuce gates left ajar no doubt
Where heaven's veil is spun

He lashed and he beat, and he lashed
"Oh Damn the lead dogs quit"
The huskies refusing not moving
In the valley of 'Lucifer's Pit'

He thought of home and his loved ones
In that, whom it may concern

# Tales of the High North

If only the 'Son of Man' spare him
And this day not come his turn

The bitter cold, the bitter cold
A chill that burned like fire
Frozen hands and frozen heart
A pain of soul so dire

But strange turns make fate in the Yukon
There he fell on his knees to pray....
Soon the lead dog was up and howlin
Then yelping as if at play
Came an answering call, and there standing tall
A Mountie sleding this way

Mushing in the Valley of the Bighorn
'The Reaper' enjoining the race
Side by side neath the northern lights
The Mountie besting the pace
Now you've heard many tales of the Yukon
Still more of the gold rush greed
So came the red coated horsemen
In honor, breed and deed

The frozen man lay in the Mountie's sleigh
While the arctic owl proclaimed....
Fool of a mortal, what made you think
That sourdoughin's a game?

## The White Cougar

I would tell you the tale of a cougar white
What roams the Yukon hills
Thirsty for the blood of whatever it stalks
Yet seldom feeds on its kills

There's nothing subtle about the beast
Nor spoor from the demons approach
A deadfall log all spattered with blood
Or bleached wayward bones that lay 'bout

A tuft of fur among some gore
Proof of a pitiless nether god
Who'll not be quenched till all life is done
And the bones of usurpers lay bleached in the sun

Some have seen it and some will tell
Of a surly white cougar, a devil from hell
That hides in the drift or some subtle rift
Oh! The scent on the breeze that he smells

So wary be you tenderfoot
And southers come searching for gold
From east to west o'er valleys crest
Be mindful but not too bold
For the big white cat of the Yukon crags
Is waiting ever patiently
Fer a fool like you too slack, unguarded
Another proffer for the white cougar's larder

## Eternal Damning

Gold to feed the Sourdough's greed and where will it all end?
By wolverine fang, by hunger pang, or a wound which no one tends
My parents dear have gone ahead to the land beyond the pole
There they rest, upon flowered crest and never feel the cold

I recall, when just a lad, a tad, at night the bush wind swept
On past a cabin in a meadow still where snug and warm we slept
And now what fate has fortune bequeathed on an orphan in the Arctic freeze
Am I not worthy of a lady's love from across this ice bound sea?

Feel the cruel sting of cold, in a land where the bold, cling to the edge of life
Hoping to fill a poke or two enough for a city wife
Ah, you pitiful dolting fool you're a Sourdough can't you see?
Doomed to taste the northern wastes and roam with your mangy team

Your lady loves are long gone past at home by a roaring fire
And you will end your days this way consumed by your true desire

Can't you see you must be free to go where you
already are
To die beneath the northern lights and the heavens
twinkling stars

Dance if you wish upon a wish for the motherlode to
rise
One day back there you'd soon declare how I long for
Yukon skies
Where free from the cares of those who care too
much to be at peace
You'd cast it all off for furs so soft and return where
you'd long to be

So rattle the huskies and crack your whip sneer at the
frost demons coldly
You've a date with fate and no time to waste to tame
the arctic boldly
Let the cursed wolves growl and the blue northers
howl
The devil take his own
Your destiny's sealed to an icy deal for the wind
swept drifts are your home

## Beyond the Rainbow Bridge

There is a place beyond Rainbow Bridge
Cross meadows and dells and an emerald ridge
Where those who've touched my life now wait
With a smile and a wave at Heavens Gate

Before I see you my leave I take
With special friends a meet to make
Those impish ferrets beckon me and over the hills
we'll glide
I'll gather them up in loving haste and we'll cross to
the other side

Soon to comfort and ease my fears
To dry my eyes of welling tears
As oft they did through pain and strife
They'll lead me into the afterlife

Into my pocket the little one climbs
While up on my shoulder another one rides
I see you all and I won't be delayed
Wait for me at the stream by the gate...
We're crossing Rainbow Bridge

Is Father there, my brother and friends?
It isn't far Mother I see the end
We won't linger here I'll soon be there
We're over Rainbow Bridge

*Inspired by the story of The Rainbow Bridge.*

## Kootenay Jack

Now Kootenay Jack was a cursin cuss
Loathed by the Caribou gals
He lived at the head of the Selkirk Range
And he kept pretty much to himself

Greed was all his black heart knew
His only love was gold
An Indian child and her kin lay slain
By a slew foot Grizzly he told

But McKenzie and Finch of the Mounted
Horsemen determined and true
They'd not bide a day
Till they'd captured their prey
For the children and cubs he slew

Wo'ojeena the she bear
Fifteen foot tall and fierce
A ten acre body with claws like knives
In vengeance her heart was pierced

They tracked him up the Nechako
On his horse he sat frozen in fear
And lying  Kootenay wove a tale
That would bring the devil to tears

But McKenzie the Mountie bound him
To the fort by the southern slope
Misty the Malamute leading to
Kootenay's date with the rope

From his perch he gazed his hair upraised
At the rites of 'Rendezvous'
Beyond the ramparts a slewfoot bear
Reared up and echoed her roar
As if to curse old Kootenay
When he dropped through the gallows door

**In Praise of Mike Doyle's Mayo**
*a sourdough tale....*

Mike left his home for the Yukon
Intent on panning gold
He laboured each day with his huskies and sleigh
But never complained of the cold

At night the wind howled and the wolves would
growl
Leery, cautious, and sly
He'd roll up cozy and warm by the fire
His lead dog and rifle nearby

Mike pondered but never made out
Why game was sparse all round
No fleeting glimpse of bearded hare
Nor pad of grizzly he found

No geese or ducks, no owl or mouse
Nor kick at a wary fox
So strange it seemed, where wildlife should team
Driven off by his larder box?

For tied to his sleigh, and hidden away
Were jars of venting gas
Tanning the hides and burning the eyes
Weeping through quarter inch glass

I'll never starve he'd chuckle
Though nature withholds at a whim
Mike's homemade mayo was just the thing
That fueled and kept him trim

# Tales of the High North

One day there appeared a Mountie
Sick as a boiled owl
Oozing sores and all a fever
His shallow breath raspy and foul

He ranted all night bout his southern home
How a mother's face glowed in the light
The fever burned and Mike was sure
He'd never last the night

Just a few leagues north a settlement
The Mountie struggled to tell....
Where the fever had struck like a demon
Let loose from the depths of hell

Sourdough Mike sat all through the night
In the pall of the midnight sun
Feeding the Mountie his mayo grand
Awaiting the coming dawn

Mike opened his eyes and to his surprise
The Mountie spry as a fawn
I don't know how you cured me Mike
I'll be damned if the fever ain't gone

The mayo they both knew
Had cured the killer flu
At break of day they tore away
To do what they had to do

Then cross the wastes a chorusing wail
And corpses all afire
Headed for heavens sleuce gates their souls

On the smoke of that ghastly pyre

They needed old Doc Finch whom....
They'd regrettably been forced to lynch
And a gambler's debt was paid
For too many aces he'd played

With the Fort Norman Doctor snowbound
They'd never last till spring
Mike and the Mountie never despaired
For they had just the thing

Now Mike Doyle's mayo is famous
All the way to the arctic pole
He's likened to Ulysses and Bachus
And oft his story is told

You can talk of Dan McGrew
And tales of the gold rush days
Of knife 'n claw and fights that was fi't
In all those awful ways

The one the Sourdoughs each recall
And raise their glasses in reverent praise
On Saturday nights at 'The Tenderloin'
....is Mike Doyle's cure-all Mayonnaise

## Yukon Kenney

They called him Yukon Ken, a special breed of man
Cabin fettered for two whole winters high in the
arctic wastes
He'd been up there so long where the north winds
flail and blaze
He'd lost about half his senses and all of his social
grace

Nary a female like what's found in "The Nugget" to
ease the strain of the trail
Just whistling wind in a constant din on a raging
deafening scale
The sourdough was all alone moilin and hackin fer
gold
Those arctic nights neath the northern lights on the
barren scapes so cold

Yukon Ken had lost all sense, of just what a lady was
He dragged himself to the Nugget Saloon, home of
sin and lust
Where those scented 'Belles' were plying their wares
Fishin fer sourdough dust

Slyest of all, the Belle of them all that cagey
Goodnight Marie
He saw her first as he walked in the door
Prancing the 'mukluk shoo' laying waste to a
deadbeat's face
Who'd cheated her of a sum that was due

Now that's the gal for me, this Goodnight girl Marie

She don't have the scent of a sourdough
By gar she sure smells good... (said Ken)
But just what should I do?

Now a one eyed 'n scarred up Fin, tried to speak
above the din
You got the rovin eye I see for the widowed belle
Marie
Well that gal loves the lure of a song can you croon
and do a tune?
I'll do my best above the rest these unwashed mukluk
shoon

He went to his sleigh, where hidden away
A Swede saw all shone and sheen
'Twas the instrument he would ply
To catch the ear and turn the eye
Of the scented Nugget Queen

An ungodly screech and scratch ensued
Everyone froze not a soul could move
While bow scraped steel in a Yukon reel
As the love in the Sourdough rose

My wealth is yours to plunder, my heart is yours to
break.
Come along with me 'Goodnight Marie'
And love me for just love's sake

Now this gal Marie had an eye for a catch
She'd bait and tell him anything he wished
For Cheechako dust or cold hard cash
It really didn't matter

And so does fate turn the wheel
In time their love was sealed
Sourdough twins a scamperin cross the cabin floor
with glee
The pride and joy of Yukon Ken
and the Belle 'Goodnight Marie'

## Star Shower

There were strange odd lights in the sky last night
As I lay by a snowridge crest
Aglow it seemed in a great light beam
And I thought that 'twas heaven's breast

The moon had bore a tunnel, through clouds
Of gossamer down
And I dreamed I was back in a cabin warm
In a valley snug and sound

Lulled near sleep by the patter of little feet
That once made our shack a home
I awoke it seemed at first from my dream
To discover I was alone

Only to wish for what could not be
For my youth was spent a moilin
In streams of water as cold as ice
I panned and I sleuced till the near fall of night

On the morrow another valley and dim
Where snow devils whirl to the canyon's rim
Sunk to my waist in search of the place
And a hope of yellow salvation
Hid from the eyes of those who seek
Since the very first day of creation

North by nor'west trudge the moilers
Clear to the polar edge
Though Franklin sleeps in the arctic deeps
Aaaaah!  he lacked a sourdough's pledge

As long as gold lay close afoot
Ne'r to quit the trail
Day after day from spring till fall
When the skies fill with snow clouds a'sail

Scrape' n scratch the frozen land
Toss and shake the dirt of the seam
Hoping for gold to just gain a hold
of the comet's tail and dream

## The Otters

Have you ever seen the otters at play
As they jink about and slide
With glee along the sleuce they go
And blissfully they glide

To splash in the water and kick without rest
To tease the beaver and wolf in jest
Foxier than the fox, and swifter than any fish
Drifting upon their backs they go in wondrous
peaceful bliss

Those bright eyed little imps
Their cunning knows no bounds
The limits of their playfulness
 Is nowhere to be found

Tawny fur a shinin
Stretched out in the noon day sun
Nimble minds never idle
 A life of mischief and fun

And who would not gaze in jealousy as...
Mother Nature's clowns parade
Frolicking Otters I envy you
Your careless days at play

## Guardian of the Right

T'was dusk on a crisp autumns' eve and a chill lay in
the air
I'd camped by the Jackpine River tossing aside my
cares
From up in the Athabasca trace
I'd wandered my way down here
In search of gold dust and furs I'd come
For I sensed at hand those riches near

When I spied a Mountie on horseback atop a crag
upstream
In a bright scarlet tunic, his majestic countenance
manning
...an eternal vigil it seemed

He'd waved but ignored my bidding
to visit and sit by the fire
To partake of my larder'n spin some yarns
For such is the custom here in these parts

He was there as the daylight fell into night
And I sank in a peaceful sleep
Unconcerned with the outside world
Wrapped in dreams soft and deep

And in the morn he still sat his mount
He'd been there unmoving all night
So again I tried to wave him down
Unflinching, a statue, the Mountie rooted stonelike

Though I hollered and waved my black skillet pan

# Tales of the High North

It appeared he'd refused to give in
Possessed of an iron will he stood fast
Above the canyon's din

I lodged a complaint when two days next
I arrived at the detachment fort
I'd thought Mounties would jaw with folks
And were always a friendly sort

The Sergeant looked me over askance...
"No Mountie patrolled the chutes anymore, all were
confined to the post
The one you saw has been there for years and in your
presence a ghost
For his roaming spirit rides alone upon the piney hills
Back shot from his mount by a retch
Ambushed as he sleuthed the trail

But every once in awhile he's seen guarding
The chutes at the rapids crest
Clean of spirit and good I must be
For he haunts only felons who pass
Every now and then a weary traveller
Or half breed stumbles in
Telling this same tale of a ghostly Mountie,
an apparition,  perched on the canyon's rim

He's waiting there for eternity ever guarding the right
Till the day of the big clean up comes
When heaven's sleuce gates spill and boil
The treasures of paradise each to their due
The end of time and life's cruel toils
For us what digs and pans and moils

## The Angel Belle

The sawdust was scattered and bloodied, o'er the
floor of the 'Motherlode'
From far and wide and all around to Dawson Creek
they'd rode
The moilers had come to toss their poke
To sing and dance and hear a joke
To drink the iceworm cocktail and spin a yarn'er two
To win or lose a fortune with the unwashed mukluk
shoon

That was the sight that greeted me
And the boys were rippin for fun
For this is what Friday night was like
in the land of the midnight sun

'Step'n a Half' and 'Hatchet Face'
Two Metis that everyone knew
They'd mushed their way for two cold days
A' scentin the devil's brew
By end of night they'd both be tight
Asleep neath the big stuffed bear.
To awake come morn, their heads held sore
Relieved of cash and cares

But first would come the drinking and then there'd be
a fight
Not for any particular cause for this was Friday night
The time it was to whoop and yell and tell a bunch of
lies
To see the dandy's try to stand a drinkin none too
wise

The moilers and jacks would draw their knives and
insults would fly about
Closing in and with a clashing rush they'd slash n'cut
n'shout
Those fights was fi't in awful ways and many brave
deeds was done
But devil take em no one cared for this was all great
fun

A voice descending sweet, it fell from gentle lips
And all the boys stood silent, a gawking - hands on
hips
An angel had landed in their midst or most of the mob
believed
Her song began slow and low and every ear was
cocked

She sang of a Mother whose heart was broken
By the sins of a wayward son
And many a tear was swiped with a brush
Of buckskin from misted eyes that shone
She tore their souls and crushed their hearts
As she sang her song of home

Guilt was rife among sinners that night
In the bright glow of wagon wheel lamps
Sourdough, half breed, each jack a man
Swore on their bond and stamp
Their days of lechery, hooch and girls
Would end this night right then

The angel departed and silence reigned
The mob was lost in thought

Till snake eyes Cooper brought them out of their
stupor
"Four aces, hell look what I got"
He waved his hand and swore to be damned
"So let the games go on"

Blood 'n hooch and cursin was rife
It continued till dawn in damnation
There were years ahead, good times to be had
And plenty of time for... salvation

## The Deer Camp Queen

She wore size twelve gum boots
And they called her uncouth
Shaped like a crate with a
Nice set of tooth

She could gut and quarter
Skin and tan
Tough as a varmint
And fight like a man

'Tis said she took a shinin
To a little feller once
But he spurned her
And broke her heart

She cried to her Pa
Till her brothers they came
The poor little feller
Was never seen again

Hands awash with blood
Her buck knife agleam
You've got to respect that girl
For she's the deer camp Queen

## Dawson Creek

Skirting the Peace River District
I made it to Pouce Coupe by dusk
I'd hole up here till the snow had cleared
Then 'twas Dawson Creek or bust

The land was flat for a mountain man
Just a few rolling hills and bumps
I loaded my sleigh and set out on my way
To top Bear Mountain by noon

The blizzard eased as I set out
 But the clouds was low to the ground
The huskies reeled and snapped and whined
Barking as we wheeled around

At the crack of the whip my curs were off
Cutting the biting cold
This is the north she eats the weak
And respects but the brave and bold

On you mutts of mange and fang
On you Hades spawned
Pull and strain and take the pain
On you huskies into the maw

See the ice worms dance and the snow devils prance
It's on to Dawson Creek
Though its dark round here this time of year
It's late till the sun truly peaks

The stars slipped in and out of the clouds

But those that showed was so bright
Although it was almost ten of the morn
It felt all the same like night

We never stopped, we only pressed on
The mountain base was clear
And the huskies must have sensed it
That the town was very near

In an hour we stood overlooking the plain
Hard for words to speak
But its downhill now in an hour or so
We'll be in Dawson Creek

It's always been a kind'a hub for Sourdoughs passing through
To rest up, grub up, and hooch up, before heading out to the slew
A place to warm yer shanks, a place to stop on the arctic flanks
Oh how we need a better trail clear true and through to Fairbanks

But now I'm here where the crossed trails meet in the centre of the town
I'll find a room at the rooming house and bed my huskies down
'The Digger Saloon' is jumping with gals of tainted repute
Some are pretty and some are as ugly as my old malamutes

But I didn't come to Dawson Creek

# Tales of the High North

To meet God's sainted best
I came to tame the wildlands
And stand the mountains crest

O'er wind swept plains and roiling streams, on and on
and on
Through gulch and canyon, blizzard and squall up
each day by dawn
Frost bite, fang bite, oh my skin is leathered and wan
But I'll suffer daily hunger pangs, I'll pass off all
comforts beyond
Until I reach the mountain break and the gold fields...
of the Yukon

## Moose Cakes
...based on a true story

Me'n Paddy Ryan was out on the barrens one spring
day
Up to our knees in boggy mud and we'd pretty much
lost our way
We wasn't new to the northern wastes alas we'd
wandered from the trail
Little concerned bout the lessons we'd learned for we
was both hardy and hale

Then of a sudden...
The bog was a'froth and a mountain did grow
And just what it was we did not know
The stocks of wild rice were parted and swept aside
Before we'd caught a glimpse of the moose's soaking
hide

He examined us both a'snorting he turned
And swam off in disdain
And as he did my stomach croaked
Then a light went on in my brain!

"Get the canoe and a stout rope too
He'll do no mischief while he swims"
Though Paddy stood gawking, confused and vexed
"Move quickly now boyo and I'll show you what's
next"

"We'll throw a noose around his rack
 And pull our canoe right up his back
 And with the axe we'll give him a whack

# Tales of the High North

And it's 'bog moose cakes' for lunch"

So we paddled out in hasty haste
Catching him up real fast
Paddy tossed the noose o'er his rack
And hauled us right up on his muscled back
But just as he was about to whack
The moose's hooves touched ground

He was off and running at a full out pace
Dragging the canoe in his boiling trace
Knocking down saplings like twigs in his wake
Branches snapping and whipping my face

Paddy and me held on for dear life
In wide eyed terror and torment
Bouncin'n bumpin o'er rocks and logs
Expectin to die any moment

The next thing I knew I awoke on the ground
And bits of canoe lay there around
I moved a toe and the rest came slow
Till I managed to crawl to a mound

In a wobbly state I arose from my fright
Paddy lay silent bruised from his flight
"Are yer dead Paddy," I asked real slow?
Says he, "Well damn it, I don't really know"

You'll hear many tales of the barren wastes
And some of them is true
Whether this one's the gospel truth or a yarn
...I leave it up to you!

## Them Damn Beaver
...based on a true story

How my grandmother hated the beaver
Bank beaver, lake beaver, river or pond
Grandma made no distinction, she wanted them all
gone

The Beaver is a builder, nature's engineer
Rerouting a shallow trickling stream in a flash a lake
appears

They'd flooded the road and flooded the yard
And Grandma was fit to be tied
She wished the trappers would trap them all
And someone tan their hides

Early one spring the beavers a plenty dammed every
runnel and stream
When grandma saw the destruction they'd wrought
She cursed and hollered and screamed

Just look what them damned beaver did
The village all awash you saw!
See it's rising still the road is gone
There's no way to get to Mattawa

We'll never make it to church through this
We're going to need an ark
You wait until I have a word
With those Rangers of Algonquin Park

Now Grandma had her knitting in a basket on the
porch
Her favorite rocking chair was gone
And never seen no more
The beaver'd downed the shade trees
And the rake from the outhouse door
All of these had disappeared about a a week before

Sternly she stood her sacred ground, against the
woodland castor
She caught a glimpse of her knit basket shiftin
And I've never seen her move faster

The beaver hissed, Grandma's cane swung and
missed
She'd get him with her broom
She swung again with all her might
And the beaver snatched that too

It takes some time for the run off to subside and risen
tempers too
Just don't take it personally if this should happen to
you

**The Bear in Grandma's Lye**
...based on a true story


An old black bear hung around for years
On the fringes of Grandma's place
We never paid him very much mind
And he'd just go on at his play

Now Grandma clung to the old fashioned ways
As elders are want to do
She had her practiced mind set
And shrugged off most of the new

Every spring she'd fill the barrel to full
With water and wood ashes too
Making her homemade lye soap
Was her own special task to do

No one ever dared interfere
Or suggest some store bought brand
For this is the way her ancestors did it
When first they cleared the land

The mix would sit for week upon week
Fermenting in the springtime sun
Bubbling, venting, surging and curing
Until the mix was done

But late in the golden afternoon
A day before it was ready
That old black bear came sniffing
 Cause he was starved and hungry

# Tales of the High North

You see lye is made with animal fat
And somehow he'd caught the scent
He lifted the lid and began to eat
Hardly getting as much as he'd meant

Now lye once steeped is fat no longer
It's soap; and each day the stew grows stronger
The bear mogged it down and then turned around
To face grandma's wrath, for she'd caught him

"Grandma watch out," we yelled
She ignored us and just didn't care
She swung her trusty corn husk broom
"Take that you thieving bear."

That broom fairly cracked on the bruin's nose
You'd thought he'd been stung by a bee
We held our breath, the bear tore away
And Grandma danced with glee

That night as we lay us down to sleep
From the forest a groan raised our hair
The lye had given him a belly ache
...and that's the last we heard of the bear

## The Wild Heart

I have a wild heart it seems
And strange blood in my veins
Each morn I long to be somewhere else
Where the sun at setting reigns

I was born to roam and wander
Never to den someplace
Never to know the vows of love
Or a bride in beautiful lace

I can't seem to set my roots down
No matter how I try
For me it's the snowy mountain peak
And want of a brand new sky

I have to see the grizzly sow
With her spring cubs at her side
The stellar jay and eagle
On the breezes where they glide

I have to swing my paddle
Through waters never broken
Calling out in canyon places
Where seldom a word was spoken

I know there's another valley
Beyond this grassy plain
Where the river teems with otter and fish
Battling the rapid's refrain

The mossy crag has been my bride

# Tales of the High North

The snow her flowing lace
And all of nature's beauty
My lover's gentle face

You have to see it's plain to me
That I will never nest
My weary soul calls out to go
When I'm dead there'll be time to rest

## The Wolverines

There's a nasty critter of the Klondike hills
Mean as a lard covered weasel and
 ...oh how it loves to kill

Carcajou the wolverine
Or skunk bear folks call them too
Reapin chaos on all in their path
For want of better to do

Now I'd always thought they was kinda cute
Playful and graceful, not really the brute
...like folks here about had claimed

A pair of them lived in a lair nearby
And their carefree antics caught my eye
Sometimes I'd laugh till they made me cry
Not sensing the danger they posed

They'd never done me or mine a bad turn
But eventually all good favor was spurned
And the cruelest of lessons I soon learned
From the fangs of the wolverine

I'd trundled down to the stream for some trout
I wasn't gone an hour
I came back to my cabin innocently
And the first thing I saw was the flour

All the contents of a fifty pound bag
Scattered about with the torn burlap rag
...but this was not the worst of it

# Tales of the High North

At the cabin door where I now stood
I took in the scene and...
It wasn't good

My home a shambles a horrid disgrace
Milk and eggs layin about the place
Pots a tumbling and rolling about
The havoc continued till I gave a shout

Those wolverines were still raisin hell
My nostrils took in that rancid smell
Their presence an omen that didn't bode well
And the time had come for the fight

It's said of these vicious hoary beasts
They neither give nor beg quarter
I was of that very same mindset
Intending to fight all the harder

I'd heard they'd battle a full growed bear
Still I had to get them out of there
And by whatever means... I didn't care

That's when I reached for my gun...
I fired they moved
I fired they moved
I fired once again
Blasting holes in my cabin floor
Till the gun wouldn't fire no more

They snorted and growled
And then they charged
A fang sank in my calf

I howled retreating, trailing my blood
Running for my raft

So a tough lesson learned
The cabin was theirs
Remember this if you see them
Well meaning like me and true as you want
You can't reach a truce with those demons!

## The Bitter Run Trail

*...no rest for the wicked.*

He rode at a gallop to the 'Bitter Run Trail'
Hoping to get away
As each sun rose to the north he'd gaze
And there those Red Coats still followed each day

He'd back shot one of their members
Near Winnipeg just awhile back
He'd always been lawless so now he ran
With the Mounties hot on his track

T'was a hard ride that he'd been making
From those who never quit
From those who'd follow relentless
A'holding to their grit

The North West Mounted were after him
Though often hard to define
He was sure that sometime early that morn
He'd crossed the invisible line

From Canada rode the Mounted Police
The west their mission to tame
The scarlet plague was after him
Like a wolf pack chasin game

He was plumb wore out near Pembina
Not holding out much hope
But runnin for him was a better choice
Than the hooded hangman's rope

They were minutes behind, his horse ran and ran
They crossed the border the Yankees be damned
 True to their motto... "to get their man"

But he couldn't seem to shake them
Like ghosts in hot pursuit
By the time they reached the 'Lonesome Pine'
Their doggedness bore them fruit

They captured the felon and quenched his thirst
"But I haven't slept," said he!
"After the gallows there's plenty of that
you've a date with eternity"

"I respect those men in their scarlet coats
Even though I'll swing on the Hangman's rope
They caught me up fair, the lesson is plain
You don't kill a Mountie and rest again"

No pearly gates but the torments of hell
I've earned the devil's due
So here I wait in the Winnipeg jail
And this is the end of... the Bitter Run Trail

## The Bear

*or…I'm gonna get that Grizz…*

T'was eighteen 'ot and ninety three when a grizzly
bear took my leg from me
He left me bleeding and screamin in pain I swore my
vengeance I'd be back again
That foul breathin beast should be easy to find cause
he's also missin a leg just like mine
I took it off with a forty four bore right above the
knee
So he limps around awkward and stumbling just the
same as me

…I'm gonna get that grizz!

I'd  bin tracking that bruin for nigh on a month
When we met head on in the Yukon trace
He showed no fear and neither did I
Till he let loose a roar and I let out a cry…"One of us
is gonna die!"

…and I won't quit!

His big hump bristled and his ears went down
Takin two long strides we went to town
And a fight to the death commenced
I cut, he clawed, gnashing and grittin his fierce grizz
jaws
One to one and me no gun
He knew he was fittin a real fight

…he wouldn't quit!

I swung my tomahawk he swung his front paw the
only one he had left
I slashed with my knife what a gory sight
We fought three days and we fought three nights
He hit me some smacks with his claws like scythes

…but I wouldn't quit!

Alas we both lay down wore out
And us were tuckered right through to the bone
Lickin our wounds with some grunts and groans
I said, "bear it's just no use"

…I won't quit if you won't!

So we cooled our cuts in a mountain stream
And I took old grizz back home with me
Sitting at the table partaking of a jug
We sat there drinking till the early dawn
And finally sleep took hold
I woke up later and the bright sun shone there was no
grizz and my jug was gone

Why that thief…I'm gonna git that grizz!

## Blue Northers
...or the journey of Sam McGee


There's a cold chill wind that blows in the north
From the arctic pole
To the plains below
And it cuts through the Sourdough's fur

The fire in the stove just couldn't keep up
With the surging gale around me
Wild and crude
Fierce and rude
Wasting in a fell storm's lee

Pellets of ice whipped and cut a cold cannonade in
my face
Of food in the larder to warm my gut there was barely
a thimble trace
Oh! my lips were cracked and scabbed.
I chewed my tongue from longing because...
Track soup was all that I had

My buffalo robe was worn and holed and frozen to
my legs
I called on God for salvation prayed and wept and
begged
My mongrel dog an ice crystal heap against the
leaden sky
I was cursin 'The Reaper' certain before the morn I'd
die

My eyes and ears bled and I seemed half dead
The hoar frost coating the hood on my head

# Tales of the High North

My fingers were froze and most of my toes
Damn! how I hated the cold

Have you ever tried to shelter in the sights of an arctic
gale?
That howls and plays nasty tricks with your mind
While it blasts and rips and wails

There came a welcome visitor, about a fortnight back.
He was blown in by the Blue Norther winds
...a tearin at my shack

Then said I...
I'll not survive nor get out alive can we make it to
Lake Laberge?
Sled me to the Post of the North West Mounted and
I'll give you all my furs
My name is Sam Magee and I came here lookin fer
gold
But all I got in all these years is cold, colder and cold

So when the thaw of spring comes and I hope it's
soon you see
I'm leaving the north on the first scow out for my
home in Tennessee

## The Night Before I Died

The northern lights gleamed, as I gazed on the scene
In the lap of the strangest sky
Peeking out of my hood at my husky brood
When I heard a white owl cry

The stillness deceiving, bespeaking peace
Across the barren scape
I wondered and dreamed by the iced over stream
Thinking upon my fate

T'was easy to reflect on the past but alas
The future is ever unknown
I wandered and pondered all through the night
And yet no wind had blown

Strange and amiss near the pole like this
Where a maelstrom always cried
But now it is morn and I don't feel reborn
So I guess the truth is I died!

## Spirit Of The North

Piney, sweet scented, blue skies surrounding
Wildlife and wild rugged spaces abounding
But the 'Spirit of the North' can't be seen

It's something that moves inside the soul
Something that grabs you and doesn't let go
...once you've felt her touch

A whispy wind in the springtime melt
An uncertain something: real, I have felt
...that moves within my heart

The spirit moves in all that lives
It moves in ways which nature gives
 ...Orendas among the spruce

Hear the mourn of the loon, the night owl croon.
One at the dawn and
...one neath the moon

This is the north, she's majestic and cruel to all in her
gaze
She leads them through and into the maze
...giving her secrets freely

Her grip is held firm on the 'Souther's' soul
She leads and lures them to the fringe of the pole
Captured, you're part of the north

Embrace her hand, her gentle heart
Go forth, go forth

# Tales of the High North

...in the 'Spirit of the North'

## Badger The Mountain Man

'Badger the Mountain Man' surly and gruff
Chompin his bacci, grizzled and tough
Livin hard by the high windy Chilkoot Pass
Trappin up beaver for the privileged class

His trader tomahawk, buckskins'n fur
The marks of a mountain man aloof and sure
With his black powder, lead throwin, smoke pole gun
He'd drop the swiftest before they could run

He'd lived with the Cree, the Blackfoot, and Sioux
The Crow, the Blood, and the Peigan too
A freer man it was hard to find...
'Badger the Mountain Man', one of a kind

He knew the ways of the grizzly and moose
The bobcat, the cougar and the wolverine too
All the things in nature he knew
Quiet, accepting of the lot that he drew

Now mountain men live with no ties that bind
They're eyes wide open they never pass blind
Happy to live for the blue sky or white
Happy to lay neath the stars of the night
The morning dew is the wine of the dawn
It freshens the spirit enriching his song

But there comes a time when the journey must end
The last 'Rendezvous' when the body is spent
His friends will gather and say goodbye

When 'Badger the Mountain Man'... ascends to the
sky

## Jenn Of The Dirk

A boom town saloon was the 'Klondike Moon'
And how I patronized it
I'd go ever when, I'd a hankerin yen, for a dram
And the card play inside it

There was Shanghai Pete, Maddawg Milligan, Digger
Dawson and me
Cursin and jokin, swillin and playin a hand
Bilkin the toll, stiffin the good, cheatin and lying
Whenever we could

Now 'Jenn of the Dirk' was one of those girls
That drift in now and again
Quick with a joke while she grabbed for yer poke
And no one knew her real name

You could kiss her cheek and touch her calf
But you dare not let yer hand slip too high
For further on up was a wee highland knife
Up in the garter tucked next to her thigh

So we named her 'Jenn Of The Dirk'...

Then one Friday night when the patrons was tight
And the Sourdoughs whooped it up
A dude walks in he was playin the pimp
A snake of the gold rush trail

Many's a young lass has been led astray, wayward
they've gone
By the likes of this knave

# Tales of the High North

I knew him from Skagway and a past black as night
When he'd killed a fair fetcher with a hidden knife

Now Jenn of the Dirk was a girl of the night with a
gentle heart few'd seen
Though often it was I acted the fool, she'd always
been kind to me
I thought I saw him droolin, I thought I saw him
longing, I thought I saw him moving
And it got my Irish up

He had the kind of face that sneered, fitted with coal
black eyes that reared
A natural dislike from those he met
I rose from my chair brushed a paw through my hair
Intending to knot his chin

I bucked up my nerve, he wouldn't have her
And I busted him upside the head
He didn't fall down he turned half around
And I watched wide eyed while he bled

Now a sucker punch is the coward's way
And I felt awful guilty right away
As I reached to steady the snake at bay
I heard 'Jenn of the the Dirk' tearily say...
Oh my goodness...
Father!

## Wintertide

Alone I abide at Wintertide
Why they call it that I don't know
Most of the time it's windy and snowin
And up here the tide is frozen!

Wintertide! a conundrum to me
As the wind rips in from the Beaufort Sea
I burrow down in my furs like a mole
Hanging on for my life to the fringe of the pole

The Snowy Owl and the Arctic Fox
Both know the north wind well
But nature made them to live with the freeze
Where a wind chill of forty below's a spring breeze

The great white bear loves to bathe in a bath
 Surrounded by blocks of ice
 Swimming about as he chases the seals
 And he thinks it ever so nice

But when the wind fouls that it makes the wolves
howl
And the iceworms wiggle and dance
When the cold burns a brand, like fire on the hands
When the muskox circle in a wind shielding stance
When the ice is so frozen it crackles and snaps
And the northern lights leap cross the Polar Cap

These are the signs that it's cold outside
 In your cabin warm you best sit tight
 Stay by the fire for it's months of the night

# Tales of the High North

And wait for the spring and the daylight

Time for a letter to old friends back home
Tell them you're fine even though you're alone
Read the worn books that wait on the shelf
And reflect on the life you live with yourself

The irony of it!

Only a Souther all kidding aside
Would call hibernation... Wintertide!

## The Fight at The Caribou Saloon

There were whisper hawks 'n tomahawks and trader
hatchets too
Knives 'n bloody fists 'n mitts, in the 'Caribou
Saloon'
Someone had started the nasty brawl, but who it was
no one recalled
It didn't matter anyhow... the last man standing took
all

The fists did fly like larks in the sky
There was hair'n skin stuck to the floor
But the Mounties were taking no guff tonight
As they charged through the oaken doors

The 'Old Days' are over the Corporal yelled, there'll
be no more of this
He made his point on a Sourdough's head with his
massive Irish fist
Now some Southers who hadn't been here long
chose to ignore our good advice
They didn't give a Digger's damn for those who
'Maintain the Right'

It was toe to toe and blow fer blow
The devil bolted for hell
There followed a crash and din therein
And came the occasional scream and yell

There are generally rules of fisticuffs they call the
gentleman's way

In the Yukon back in them bad old times, that wasn't
how they played
Nose bitin, ear bitin, knives and clubs or whatever
came to hand
And in a 'Caribou free for all' this was how you made
your stand

There were twenty grizzled men of the north
With six big Mounties giving forth
And so the fight was fit...
The sawdust there that lay about served as an early
bed
For each broken man left bleedin, nursin his battered
head

Screamin'n cursin the battle ensued and neither side
gave ground
But alas all good things must reach an end so all of us
sadly found
For when the racket settled
And silence gave way to relief
The only ones left standing there were...
The North West Mounted Police

## Spurs and Red Serge

There comes a time in life to purge
To lighten the tasks
To hang up the spurs
To rack the stetson
And the faded red serge

My gold striped trous' don't fit like they should
And I don't stand as straight as I once stood
It's time for writing and days recounted
Bout my early years with the North West Mounted

Yes, it's quiet time by a roaring fire
To tell of the days when we never tired
Of a force in the north that would quickly gain fame
In the lawless days when first we came

Sit tight Lad and feed the fire another log
Sidle up there beside 'Misty' my dog
I'll tell you tales of the wilds uncrowned
And the great herds of buffalo all around
Of many days spent - on the track, on the scent
In the knife edged Yukon hills

Hear my words of valorous deeds
And the felons that we found
Like an unyielding blood hound in hot pursuit
When we rode evil doers to ground

When the noble chiefs gathered their tribes
And owned it all from sky to sky
Those days on the trail and the long patrols

# Tales of the High North

And the villains that we chased

The young ones today sit wide eyed in wonderment
In the glow of the tales that are told
And how by honor a legend was born
With the Mounted men who tamed the north

Of eagles on high as they sailed in the breeze
And how our fame spread from sea to sea
Of deeds that were done when right was affirmed
By the North West Mounted Police

## Chilkoot Pass

A wall of white high stood before our eyes
And we awed in the sight from the ground to the skies
How in Sam Hill would we conquer this hill?
Trudging and climbing with a ton of supplies

The Mounties levied the border tax
And checked off each piece on our canvassed racks
Certain with each upward step we made
The loads we carried would crush our backs

Up we gazed to a blue sky above
Urging those ahead with a shuffling shove
Vertical near - the featureless slope
With each man a death grip on the guiding rope

Damned exhausting this vertical walking
It drained the body and mind
Feeling our laboring hearts nearly break
With each passing step that we climbed

We'd all of us push till the top
Defying the wind and cold
And once up there the goal down below
The scape of the Yukon'n Cheechako gold

But before the treasure was real in our hands
Before our fortunes were laid in loot
Many would die of a broken heart
In the hell freeze Pass of the Chilkoot

But we're driven on from dusk till dawn

# Tales of the High North

And ever the long line moved
Those who died had stopped mid stride
Just to catch their breath
A fatal mistake there were no breaks
Where a single misstep brings death

But alas Chilkoot Pass would fall to the bold
And those who lusted and moiled fer gold
Those who bent their backs and scratched
Who never wavered from the Stampeder's path
Burdened, determined to claim their due
The wealth of a land from the singing sleuce

## The Last Post

I last saw a flash midst a thunderous crash
And softness enfolded me round
I awoke in awe of the sight I saw
Beneath the throne of God

There stood three comrades straight and tall
Next to the Almighty in line
Under each was a plaque with their names
And the very last one was mine

I am but one of many
To find myself here t'is a mystery to me
So I take my place beside my comrades
And stand my last post
... for eternity

## Defile

The legends are rife of the first who went forth
By canoe or trackless trail
And there hapless, reckless ere to cross
The great granite shield of the north

In those ageless days their fortunes were made
Where furs did abound, gold all round
Oh the wealth they found lay there on the ground

From blousy eastern places
Sallied out for the northern traces
The boldest of all that were lured by the call
Those faceless who challenged the green forests fall

Their fate so often an unmarked grave
And a mourning heart back home
To suffer in pain through madness or fang
The riches would be their gain, and again…

Tortured and beaten and damned near eaten
Suffering natures ways
Culling their dreams from the icy streams
Stowed in their dog dragged sleighs

How often they trudged upon the path
To tame the beast of a savage land
To beat their way by any way
And means by which they can

Day after day plodding their way
The tiny craft slip west by nor'west

# Tales of the High North

Ignoring the strain from each league they gain
Exhausted at each days rest

Then it's...
Black fly, horse fly, deer fly, and tick,
Hard tack and pemmican grool
Mangey rabbit, half starved duck
And some days only deer track soup

Then Hudson Bay and again away, westward always
west
White water, still water, muskeg and chute
Through blackberry bush and buggy bog too
Till weary of spirit and shorn of shoe

Raging rivers and black water lakes
The call of the loon sublime
Driven by lust with a ingrained drive
Gravely defying the seasons in time

Broken of spirit and broken of heart
But oh how alive these venturers first
Day in day out as they sweated and cursed

At journeys end their plews stowed away
They'd struggled again to the post on the bay
Lords of all the lands they'd traversed
Free like no pommy a slave to his purse

No sweat house drudge at this verge of creation
They happenstance founded a poor man's nation
Where all are princes and kings of empire
To rise in the morn their ordained desire

# Tales of the High North

Not to wake dead and not to be e't
The face of the sun shining down
A few more pulls of pemmican
A few more pulls on the oars
Soon to each his hard won reward
A sniff of the salt chuck… of Hudson Bay shore

## The Souther

Gather, lend your ear
For the tale you're bout to hear
Of the gory Klondike goldrush days is fabled

The first snows soon were fallen
Where a gibbous moon had risen
And cast an eerie shadow
Through the dancing mists a'riven

The souther sets out twisted
Of a mind to tame the beast
Only the mountains and the vale will win
For the fates demand their feast

Upon the broken bones
Of tenderfoot soft shoon
The wolves give forth their mourning howl
Neath the hoarey peaked faced moon

A trail of woe and carnage and one lost in his path
His eyes alust fer placer dust upon an ice floe raft
Come nigh and forth good fortune
He'd die or hone 'the craft'

They sneer in contempt oho!
Here comes another Souther
To the land of the burnished flesh and hide
Skin all soft and city white

T'is said he'd tipped the boundary verge
And swam amongst the floating bergs

# Tales of the High North

And raced a big white bear as he laughed
Across the Beaufort sea
The fool had lost his head and sense
As anyone would agree

He rid a comets tail they say
From dark of dusk to light of day
O'er the thunder 'n lightnin sky and scapes
For to pan the lands beyond away

Slid down curtains of northern lights
In his woollen johns and boots
Half mad aloft above the firs
Afar t'was heard his laughter and hoots

He never found the motherlode nor peace of mind and
ease
After years of pain and toil exploring the frozen seas
And now he stands all shrivelled and cowed
Before heavens judgement seat
Anxious and pitifully weeping in the face of
uncertainty and wondering just where
Up or down?
He would spend eternity?

## The Skull Busters

A skull busting crew led by Big Claude LaRue
Came into "The Tenderloin"
Where a moment before saw the hooch rats crushed
Now not a soul spoke in the fearful hush

Claude La Rue was a Montreal boy who bullied his
way here about
In night time dreams the moilers schemed
Of how they`d someday plug that lout

But not a single one of them ever awoke that brave
Not enough to skin his holsters
For big Claude LaRue his myrmidons too
Silenced the braggards and boasters

Now Larue and his crew won every big game
Of chance without chance them stealers
For their cusses and threats fairly terrified, every faro
dealer
And never were nuggets ever laid for the Yukon
hooch they drank
They`d lift it from some poor weak broken moiler and
never utter their thanks

The Skull Buster crew weren't many but few
Still they cowed "The Tenderloin" mob
With head butt and fists by cuffs and by kicks
They'd cripple some digger and not care a lick

Then one wild evening from out of the peaks came a
plaid clad Scottish lad

Thick of thigh and thick of mane a hee'lant man of
Yukon fame
For red cropped Angus danced a reel like no other
gentleman could
On Friday nights fueled by the whiskey most often
more than he should

Now Claude laid a bet each week of gold no man
could knock him out
But note the catch t'was tit for tat and he owned the
right to payback
So our wee Scots lad was up for the dare and he told
the big man, "I'm bound"
Claude gave a laugh and turned his head to inform the
crowd around

And while his gaze was averted our laddy ascended
the bar
Smiling and grinning, reeling and spinning, dancing
along on his toes
When Claude turned round came the boot of young
Angus
And crushed the big bully's face and his nose
Deftly struck and square to his mug the skull buster
hit the floor
Not missing a step Angus fairly leapt and swiftly tore
out the doors

Our fair Scots lad got his poke of gold
And disappeared into the night
Claude and his mob never returned
Sorely a'feared to fi't a real fight

Now things are grand at "The Tenderloin"
And each week the tale is told
You can scratch your claim till it all goes bust
Or venture out with the bold
Truth be said that in the end
Takes a Scotsman to pocket the gold

*Based on a true story with some stretching that
occurred in 1971...*

## Caribou Katy

She sang and danced for the sourdoughs
On nights when the moon fairly creeped
From behind the misty skies above
Where the blue hued mountains had peaked

The Peace River jammed with slab and floe
The frozen snow snapped and cracked from the cold
Where the north wind had trimmed the sullen pines
The eerie cry of an arctic owl breaks the still of the
night

Across the wastes in their storied grace
They sledged and skied and shoed
Hell bent a'fire to drink the fire
Of the Caribou Saloon

Desperate was their mission each
To see her tresses swirl
For every moiler there in the crush
Loved the scented pearl

Oh what clowns what fools they were
Neath the glow of the kerosene lamps
Diggers and slushers, southers and mushers
And some just dead broke tramps

In a clap board hall by the forests fall
Called the 'Caribou Saloon'
Intoxicating, lilting and flirting
Katy would sing and croon

# Tales of the High North

Many the palmed akimbo kiss
From tear flecked faces tossed
From drunken sotted Klondike men
And pokes of fine panned dust

With frozen nose and blackened toes
They'd suffered the Yukon freeze
Each to have his sad heart broke
And dropped down to his knees

Now Katy's days of reverie
Of song and dance are through
The pace of age has changed her face
For time the ravager takes its due

Yet after all these years have past
Her image etched in my mind
Though nature is no respecter of youth
My own reflections are all soft and kind

Caribou Katy the only lady
And it's a well known fact
Escaped the brothels of scented sin
With her sainted soul and virtue in tact

## Toledo

So long since I heard the ring of the riggin or heard
the cry of a gull
So long since I felt the well known surge of the
ground swell on the hull
If I could only break these chains
And make my way to the rolling main
I'd never again set a dirty mark on the shores of
sunny Spain

The ladies of Spain have a way they gain, a sailor
laddie's gold
With scented tress and flowery dress
By her flashing eyes she had me
Now I rot in a castle keep longing for the oceans deep
I'd sell my soul to the devils own to wake away on a
following sea

Beware my lads of the ladies of Spain
Ladies of Spain oh those ladies of Spain
Don't swear your oath to the ladies of Spain
Or t'is certain you'll never see St Johns again

My old ship was a jacks delight
Her hull and her sheets were snowy white
But I'm layed low and I miss her so
Her lines were the best in the gales and blows.

If I'm ever loosed to the Klondike I'll go
To the wilds and places of waist deep snow
And never again give the ladies of Spain
To charm and strip me of my gold and my soul

**Sourdough Sam**

Sourdough Sam was a moiler I'm damned
From back in the Blackstone trace
Where few if any ventured nigh
By the craggy mountains face

Varlet and varmit each alike gave its passes a safe
wide birth
For tales aplenty are told of those who vanish and
never return
In a stark bleak land not fit for man
There dwelt cagey Sourdough Sam

They're called the northern mysteries, part fable part
legend too
Sum it up all the things that go wrong
Consider the fates as well
You're just a man a speck on the track
What lays in the Blackstone none can tell

One tale and old of a motherlode
And others that shouldn't be told
Where mean old Sam he sleuced and he panned
With nary a nugget to show

In tattered hides and worn mukluk shoon
Each year he staggered in
On bandied legs all bent and aching
But never it seemed his spirit breaking

One year after the passes had cleared
And the night was lit with stars

# Tales of the High North

A cunning moiler found Sams camp
By the Blackwater's silting sandbar

Sam can't be a god fearin man the moiler troubled the thought
Praying so still upon his knees everyday it seemed all day
He saw an angel raising Sam
And carried him away

And in his shack now still and silent
One wall was pressed with sacks
The moiler paused and wondered
At the labels there attached
Every single one of them read
For the orphans of Medicine Hat

Outlandish tales in the Klondike are told
Of the men who scrape and scratch for gold
Sourdough Sam was the lyingest man
To whom the maker gave breath
But he was king of the Blackstone
And he alone escaped death

**Cabin Fever**

A man can go half mad and insane when fettered to
his cabin
While the nor'westers scream like banshees in an ever
unceasing din
The ice plates rise and rattle at the frost painted lead
glass window
Till it seems the floor will lift right up from the
constant blast and blow

Day after day on any day an arctic gale will rage
Alas the digger a poor little bird trapped in an icy
cage
It isn't fit nor safe to go out so much as a step from
the door
You can't see the trees or beyond your knees
While a whiteout tears midst a blizzard's roar

The noise and din plays a sick nasty game and the
mind becomes confused
All glossy eyed as you shake and rant you begin to
laugh yet not amused
Sight and pain overload the brain and the senses soon
are addled
You've faced many bear with a devilish stare but oh
God now your rattled

There's no such thing as the lee of a storm that batters
round the clock
One curses and flails at the storm outside as defiant it
scorns and mocks
The musk ox lager the wolves den and cower

# Tales of the High North

And man not knowing that hell could freeze what a
nasty twist of fate
Damn the man that Sourdough Sam, give him Lillith
for his mate


The skeeries of the arctic north have you in their
sights
You beg and whine to your maker divine please see
my retched plight
You beseech a night of sleep and peace
Here with your husky dogs
I swear on the grave of my mother dear I'll never
again do sin or wrong


Chase the banshees from my door and lower my
cabin back onto its floor
I'll confess every damning sin I did and never sin no
more
I'm plum wore out and it's no use to shout
For nary a soul can hear me
Is this the end of my poor mother's son?
To die abandoned and all alone with no one to know
I'm gone


Please banish the storm and come the morn
On a day when there'll be no dawn
Burrow me nigh in skins warm and soft
Heal my gout and clear my cough


Lead me away to warmer climes
Where green grass grows all year
Pain me not with memories
Nor the snow demons grip of fear

And if I die neath arctic skies
Lulled by the malamute's whine
Scatter my ashes atop the hill
Beneath the lonesome pine

## Spring

There are but just two seasons in the northlands…
Winter and fall
A few weeks of warmth and a bit of a thaw
Before the dreaded freeze sets in… and that's all

Enough to spring the midges and skeeters
Voracious tiny tundra demons
Those siphoning blood thirsty man - flesh eaters
The ground wet and spongy yet wild flowers bloom
A few weeks of blessed sun and warmth
Before the winters lingering gloom

The floes afloat out on the bay
Bergs adrift upon their way
The streams a'rush with golden dust
The moiler crazed with a panner's lust

The critters too are all about and wildlife abounds
T'is new hope against all hope out on the arctic
grounds
Amidst the stunted spruce and goss
Beneath the bluest brightening sky
The digger swears just one more time
I'll not give in until I die

That poor soul has the fever sparked by placer dust
He's sledged and trudged o'er featureless scapes
To lose himself in the arctic wastes
He'll never yield though he's fussed and cussed
Admit it you fool your claims a bust

Throughout the years the hours grim
Splintered bone and scarred up limbs
That mark his labours and alter his gait
And so he`s shackled to this earthbound state
Only a shadow to those who wait

## 50 Degrees North by North

Where the cold wind blows o'er the ice and snow
In the land of the midnight sun
The legends are rife of the fight for life
Where the bravest are put on the run

Cut and run to where?
It's white in every direction
Snow blind and cursed, frost bite un-nursed
Toes sloughing off black and gored
Reaching the edge and it can't be ignored
When you're facing Lucifer's hell bound door

Across the tundra the wolf packs roam
In search of unwary fools
They'll feed on the muskox if one should stray
But a slow moving man will serve just the same

What will they say of his carcass all flayed
By white gnashing fangs when he's mauled
How he did fight neath the northern lights
But his efforts were vain all in all

When man is weak there's a nasty streak
Of nature in its course
Food are the lame, the starving, insane
On the savage wastes where the pack stakes its claim

In the land of the beasts who wander and feed
Where humans are seen as a boon in disguise
The circle shrinks and the curs pad and slink
One gleaming eye turned to the prey to their prize

One bullet left in the breach locked and loaded
For a retched soul tortured, pursued and goaded
To die buy the gun or yield to the fang
It's a horrible choice in a place left untamed

Such was ordained their fate for the fevered lusters of
gold
When no choice was left but surrender
Their bones scattered round to the echoing howls
The demons jaws, oh how they gnaw upon their
ghastly plunder

## The Shooting at the Diggers Saloon

In the "Diggers Saloon" where some wasted dame
crooned
And they paid her to please just shut up
A grudge was brewing and the gunfight ensuing
Was bound to brake up the boredom

'The Reaper' stood a'wringing his hands, sickle
resting and ready
A double header a good catch this
Now if one would just start aim steady and true
And for my poor sake please don't miss!

Their pistols raised both of them crazed
Which fool would start to shoot first
Slowly they circled eyeing each other
Steely eyed staring as each of them cursed

The Mountie unsnapped his holster flap
One flinch and you both go down
They stopped and stared at the law man…
There's two of us and you're just one
About to die by both of our guns

The first one twitched the second one flinched
We never saw the redcoat draw
As if a blur it was it seemed
For as fast as he shot
His peacemaker resaddled in his holster slot

Two men fell to the sawdust floor
And blood spewed out their heads

Both of them drilled between the eyes
And nobody doubted they both were dead

They'd called down the thunder and paid with their
lives
A foolish thing to do
When the mounties say drop em that's just what they
mean
Or yer head'll get drilled with a through and out seam

'The Reaper' exalted ...
Not three but two, oh I guess that'll do!
To them makes no iota
The pearly gates for these await
I'm only one less than my quota

*...but the day's not over!*

## The Moose that Came to Town

Now an amorous eye had a moose nearby
Who roamed the fringe of the town
People just ignored the beast
For it seemed he'd always been round

T'was Christmas time
In the year of our Lord
Eighteen hundred and eighty nine

The town was bright and festive
The children raucous and restive
Awaiting the mid winters eve

His heart beat fast for the antlered lass
That stood in the "Dry Goods" window
He saw no mate and he couldn't wait
For her big dark eyes enticed him

So at a trot he boldly sought to win the heart of the
doe
Who never moved but ever wooed
The big hulking moose to her window

People stood aghast and gawked
At the strangest of any sights
Of the ambling amorous moose
Beneath the northern lights
…headed straight for the Dry Goods Store

Then there came a crash as the window was smashed
And the great beast bounded inside

The screaming and yelling can't they leave me alone
So sad and indignant that he didn't know
For the moose was in love with a pretty stuffed doe
He stood confused, heartbroken

He turned around and deftly leapt to the snowy street
below
And with a sneer and a big moose tear
Casually strode away

So in a season if you should see a big bull moose by
the road
His antlered rack and along his back agleam with
tinsel and bulbs of glass
Well that's our moose bad tempered and spurned for
he never got the lass

## Shadow Dance

Handmade shapes on an ice cave face that dance and
run about
The caribou chased by the wolf in its trace or a snowy
owl in flight
The legends told while a harsh wind blows and
whistles in the arctic night

A theatre white in the warm fire light as the figures
shrink and grow
The big white bear and the arctic hare from hands that
shadow dance
A burrow deep in the arctic freeze while the winter
storms advance

Days on end the northern men alone on the tundra
steps
The tales they tell on the igloo walls of hunts and
visions past
A grand procession of every legend retold by the
shadows cast

The sweeping curtains of lights in the sky
The whine of the malamute there at your side
So safe, snug and warm for all is well this night

Recalled in dreams your childhood days
Ever carefree in the suns warm gaze
How find you here beyond?

A sweep of your mitt on the lanterns wick
As if some conjurers trick

By the magic of the shadow dance
You've caused the sun to set

Oh how sweet the onset of sleep
Snug like a babe just newborn
Warm at peace in your igloo keep
Adrift in dreams till morn

## Going Back

I see my journey home in all my fleeting dreams
Where I know each emerald valley and every spruce
shrouded stream
The chalk bottom creek where the wary trout hides
Laying in wait for the moss worms and flies

I'll kiss the dawn in my far off home
And seek out the faces of those I've known
The sound of the trains that awaken the valley
The rivers of my boyhood where so often I sallied

The spread of the hills the woodlands the cornfields
The woodchucks ducking back in their burrows
Beneath the hawks piercing gaze
So much I've still to remember from my innocent
boyhood days

It all paints in contrast to my cabin door scenes
Where each night I lay my head
A howling pack challenge up high in the timberline
The glacier beyond and the kingdom that's mine

My garron is old and oh sorely worn
His days are numbered and I'm certain he knows
I'm old like him and my sight grows dim
We'd both of us best hit the trails afore the snows

It's the devils wages when the passes are sealed
And far off spring but a sallow yearning
The mountains around from sky to the ground
The squirrels in the pine trees, the stellar jay too

# Tales of the High North

The crags and the rapids roaring and churning

I've tasted of paradise with the Yukon's assent
The loon and the geese the call of the moose
Known days of wonder in the dawns early mists
The mornings afire with the sun's warm kiss
All of these things I will surely miss

The tales that I'll tell to the settled back home
They'll scarcely believe I know
For all of the words in the lingo of man
Could never do justice to the vast northern lands

## Who Owns the Pole

Now the Yankees below the forty ninth line tell us
they own it too
So do the Russians, the Nords and the Swedes and
each demand their due
By what right say I do they claim the skies that spew
the northern lights
It's owned by none but the brave and the frozed
who've stood in the midnight sun

Some claimed it for kings and others for fame
Still others in some dead prince's name
Sure there's oil below and bright gold on top
Riches scattered that southers don't see
Only the diggers and moilers like me

Who is man to claim the pole
A phantasm unseen in the daring ones souls
Haunted and barren with a vicious streak
Her secrets held in an icy keep

In the arctic night the curtains of light shimmer across
the heavens
Who can own such a wonder?
The northern lights are a gift freely given
Above the unseen circle nature is queen of all
Where mans dirty footprint is soon erased
By spindrift snows like finest lace

Who would stand un-humbled before her fury and
force?

Franklin tried and beaten he died wedged in an ice
jammed course
Many are the unmarked graves that have told of the
foolish and over bold
Who gambled all in a hapless call that led them to
grief untold

Mind you man so many the damned no reverence
offered is just callous greed
You'll join the rolls of many before a casual feast for
the unseen beast
Laugh in jest like all the rest when she bends you to
your knees
Hard in her heart she'll sneer and scorn before your
suffering, begging and pleas

So low is man in nature's grasp she's no lover yours
You cannot, will not own her she can break your back
and your soul
No one can posses her she cannot be bought or sold
So tell me now if you will…
Who can own the pole?

## A Hoary Solitude

You've heard all the tales of strife and toil
Bout the men who muck and mire and moil
Dark legends are many of the dead by the trail
The echoing cry of some trapper's last wail

Not all is bleak on the rim of the pole or hard by the
arctic circle
It's often I've gazed at the peaked moons face
A peace unknown to citified folk
A quiet that seemed out of place

At times like these I'm humbled as I take in the
beauty around me
Crystal like diamonds the snow spread for miles a gift
few ever see
Perfection not a flaw, not a track to maul, what man
could never create
Nature serine lays a dazzling scene and man knows
an hour of the maelstrom in spate

So small one feels in a land laid far and further than
the eye can glean
Neath shooting stars that streak and flash and seem to
light at your feet
The cities call out
Hear the din of the streets
For all its allure it can never compete

I 49'ed straight to Fort Edmonton's line
A hard right turn to the northern spine
Struggling the greenhorn souther that I was

# Tales of the High North

Full of youthful élan, some dreams and just because

So I found the Klondike where gold was my goal
Now I'm old and worn it would seem to be
But oh so rich in my soul

The treasures I carry I'll take to my grave if I'm
granted the afterlife
My gold is the memories of valleys first trod
By no other footpad since t'was made by God

I'll recall the scent of the spruce while the bannock
slowly bakes
The snap and crack of the fire from roasting venison
steaks
The mournful cry of the loon cross the hills
The cool soft mist off the tarns and rills

A red squirrel chucking shells at me from way atop an
old gum tree
The stellar jay plotting a plundering feed
The striking bellow of the wahpati
Calling for its long lost mate
The salmon run in the springtime melt when the
rivers are all in spate.

The solitude where one can think will cure mans gold
lust greed
So tell me what it is if more… does a wandering
panner need…?

**Welcome To Tuktoyaktuk**

Tuk some say in a jesting way
Tuktoyaktuk others say
But the NCO at the Mountie post
Was not the kind to render his boast
When I asked him where are the barracks?

In the shack out back just drop your pack
A hovel of shrunken tongue and groove
I stood in disbelief…
A sad little stove and some kindling wood
Abandoned by kin and luck
With a snicker of glee he laughed at me…
Welcome to Tuktoyukyuk

Did he really mean the things he'd said
This was my home with a driftwood bed
A canvas mattress of moldy down
My face all paled with a sad mans frown
I stood aghast my gear now shucked
And said beneath my breath…
Welcome…to Tuktoyukyuk

Now there sits your dog a mangy thing
Ill tempered, aloof and nasty, no zing
He had no fleas or mongrel disease
But his belly was groaning and hungry
I feared that if ever given the chance
The mutt would feed on me

Now I hope you can fight cause Friday night
The trappers gather and brawl

Hooch and blood are their only joy down at the
'Tanners Hall'
The floor fairly shakes and the building quakes
As they dance the mukluk shoo
They swing from the rafters and lay on the floor
Dodging debris as they dash in the door

A bottle flew, here comes a boot, deftly I shift and
duck
Stepping over a sleeping dog, no wait!
It's another crawler from Tuk

I swear by all that's holy that if ever I escape this
T'is back to Regina to never complain
Of how tough garrison life is

I'll shine my saddle and shine my boots
I'll make my spurs simply gleam
It will warm my heart when I'm torn apart
By the Sargeant Major's screams

I'll clean the horse stalls clean and sweet
I'll clean away the horses muck
Just please don't ever send me back
Again to Tuktoyaktuk

## Mike Doyle's Back Again

The folks were up in arms and soon began to shout
The shelves are bare of what we need to live life this
far north
And now the rivers blocked with ice
Oh pray it shifts in timely course

An ice jam fierce had blocked the river nothing got in
or out
The children cried some elders died
We're all for the chop if we don't get supplies

Now Mike Doyle was ever a bust as a panner
No moiler or digger was he.
But his soporific concoctions
Were praised to the brink of the seas

People would often surrender their savings
For a jar of Mikes mystical paste
And many the life of a scurvied one saved
For the gorp that he called 'Mike's Mayonnaise'

The ingredients are a close guarded secret you know
He'd gained great fame with his medical mayo
Hold the jar tight and firm in your mitt
No! You don't want to know what's in it

There was no powder or dynamite
Not a stick anywhere to be found
Came Irish Mike with a sled of his brew
He'd blast the ice jam round

So they pulled Mike's jars from out of their kegs
They spanned the ice clogged chute
And the village drunk was dragged from his bunk
To risk the sparkin of the improvised fuse

Came a thunderous bang from up the canyon where a
mountain once had stood
In all tarnation he'd altered creation as if a human
could
For now not a river clear of ice but a lake for leagues
about
Although the scene was ever changed the town was
heard to shout

Of Bachus' kin and Glaucus' ilk he's saved us once
again
Here lays his claim to Yukon fame
So raise your mug or rise your cup
In praise to Mike Doyle in the cusp
…he simply loves to blow things up

## Men of the North

We men of the north have boldly gone forth
Though they say the goldrush is ended
What we seek is something not known
Though profits are few our backs broke and bended

Is it furry hides or just to abide where man can be at peace
Suffering sores and varmit gore just to touch the golden fleece?
To prove to oneself your metal battling a north sourced gale
At times to test your inner depths and conquer the lonely trail

Crowning ones self the greatest of bards who can dispute what you say?
At the top of your lungs your story is sung
Good or bad matters not who cares?
Someday it may be your claim to fame
When your sight has faded and hair turned to grey

Go ahead! sing loud, sing out of your time upon the mount…

I once spent three days on the slopes of a peak
Tent bound, hide bound and frightened oh so bad
The crash of the sloughing kept me awake
Till I thought I would soon go quite mad

The blizzard tore cross the icy face of my desperate Yukon hold

Some bannock and pemmican was all I had to stave
off the terrible cold
The winds they howled till I swore they sang of a
pyre prepared just for me
The echoing crashes sounded like demons dancing in
hellish glee

Beneath the cornice I held a death grip clutching the
rock with my nails
And all day every day I shuddered to the nor'westers
mocking wail
I swore again and cursed all sin if I could only escape
No more bug house women for me no hooch and
gambling games

Never to darken the houses of shame those scented
vixens of Yukon fame
Never to curse on Sundays or use the lords name in
vain
Now here I thought me an atheist...
Strange how a scrape with death can change this
Amazing how a man gets holy sudden like
When he feels 'The Reapers' kiss

## Mountain Fever

I caught the mountain fever when only seventeen
It snared me in its clutches when first I gazed on Lake
Louise
Around me snow capped peaks that beckoned
And piqued my curiosity
A flatland kid untethered in the heart of the towering
Rockies

The sun was shining I lay there reclining upon the
desolate face
And faced that face determined to summit by anyway
Now my ice axe sits with a nylon rope my crampons
nestled nearby
There they rest on the old book-shelf and I can only
sigh

My limbs are tired my bones all bent
My posture askew I so resent
Age the timeless ravager
My recollections salve the pain with pleasant
memories
Of a youth well spent in enterprise on those vertical
localities

I long for vistas on the peaks the world beneath my
feet
Alas and oh sometimes I sigh
This is no way for the mountaineer to wither away
and die.

Some would call it a frivolous pursuit, yet...

I've held the dying in my arms
The living in my hands
Known killing glacial gales
Learned the meaning of compassion and passion
Love and broken heart, but…
The spirit never died in me although my body fails

I've stood where Conrad Kain did
I've stood above the clouds
Although no one could hear me
 I shouted to the world aloud

For just a passing moment I was my own superior
For just a passing moment I was an emperor
Let them take away my home and all the earthly
things I own
Let them take away all these
…I'll just keep my memories

## The Duke of Lake Laberge

I hit the vein in 88 I'd found the motherlode
Folks stood wide eyed and gawked at my lucky
fortune in gold
The assayer swooned at the nuggets in sacks
I'd brought to Dawson on my strong mules backs

A note of credit was written for me
And I lit out striding to cash in my dreams
South as the crow flies to Medicine Hat
And proceeded to go on a spree

Only the finest rooms and fair
I pampered myself without any cares
Often I drifted in waking dreams
And gazed upon those northern scenes

I spent and spent and still rich as sin
I packed the civilized spaces in
Thus ending of my wanton rich man's spree
Hustling back to Lake Laberge
Made famous by Robert's Sam McGee

I built a home for all of those
Who failed to drift the motherlode
Or struck it rich like me
So not a one would end his days in destitution and
shame
For something touched my soul deep down
And what was I to gain?

My fellow moilers meant so much

I couldn't turn away
We'd raise the place together
Thus all could stake their claim

A simple home I built nearby and there I'll await the
cleanup
When the last day comes on the wakin up morn
I'll face the angels humble and bowed
For sharing t'is said is the greatest of gifts
And I gave all I had to the Lake Laberge crowd

## The Barrens Grip

The Barrens are glacier scraped smooth and
undulating
Stagnant pools of still black waters and vistas
unrelenting
Stunted spruce, muskeg and varmit
To most a land that God has forgotten
To others a place where few have trodden

At first glance dead like some desolate desert
But so easy the eyes are misled
For life abounds and all around
Natures gifts lay hidden

Muskrat, beaver and barren moose lay claim to
leagues beyond
Even the blackfly and midge hold a place
Beneath the sky the ravens call across the barren
wastes
The ermine slinking its speed unmatched
Seeking the lair of some coney
Oh! How cold the nor'westers blow
And oh how the wolverines revel

Humans cleave to the comforts they need
Each to his own in measure
For only man adds up his gains
By degrees and sums of leisure

But hard and bold stand these men to the blows
Struck by a land unforgiving and cruel
No venue for those whose hearts are frail

No place for a civilized fool

But to those who remain and make their stand
They carry inside the ghosts of the land
Where sought for the beauty is found
In every stream by the ptarmigans call
At night neath the stars by the lone wolfs howl
All of your precious furs laid up rolled and tied and
horded
Where fair trade for peace is ordained and to man
some grace rewarded

## Claim Jumpers

I'm mean and wary, over contrary
There's claim jumpers everywhere
My breach is primed on my forty four bore
And I'm not diplomating not once no more

Four Cheechakos dead in their racks
Before they could even get out of their sacks
Drilled clean right through their heads

What kind of scurvied snake bred cuss
Would do such an evil deed?
The answer to your question friends
Is simply gold dusters greed

All the schoolin and Sunday schooling
And all that "good will to man"
Doesn't amount to a diggers damn
When the beast of greed is loose on the land

For when the fever takes them
They'll slit their best friend's throat
Steal his dogs, his golden watch
And lit out in his boat

They'll shoot their neighbour in the back
Right off his Yukon sleigh
With nary a thought of damnation
Or concern they'd someday rue the day

And many have swung from the lonesome pine
A noose about their necks

Left there as a warning to further derelicts

But my claim is mine, it is my mine
And I won't be bushwacked and slain
For I can shoot as true as true
And I'll drill them varmits through and through

Let them come call the thunder down
For I've worked too hard in the cold to fold
I'll stack their carcasses in a pit
With a sign that reads right over it
"They were overbold"

## The Pinetree Line

There flew the planes
All northward bound
And we were their eyes in the sky
On the ground

The Bears came in from over the pole
Pushing the curtain in search of a hole
But the focus was fine on the Pinetree Line
Each dish a part of the whole

Ever vigilant the Red Bear knew
Manned and scanned the duty crews
An undeclared battle of nerves and wire
And yet never a single weapon fired

So the sabres were rattled by the mighty and fine
While we kept watch
... on the Pinetree Line

## Guns of the Sundance

The gunfire rang with a crash and bang
While rococheted bullets whined and sang
T'was a dangerous unsettled truce this thing
That both sides had declared

The shots recounted had fairly amounted
To thousands and thousands 'twas said
All fired wild, as if loosed by a child
It's a miracle no one was dead

The snap and hiss of a hornet's near kiss
Will pale a man's face with fear
You feel quite alone and it's strange to know
Just briefly...'The Reaper' so near

Ambush and enfilade, ambush and skirmish
Anarchy in the Devil's lap
Out of the trees like a hail of bees
The lawless sprang their traps

The 'Renegades' had gambled
 'The Force' would run in fright
But the Mounties bound by honor
Refused to surrender...
"The Right"

This is not a Sundance,
This is not Cypress Hills or Batoche
Not the death song of 'Almighty Voice'
No one need pay the cost.

# Tales of the High North

Death it is said never validates
T'is a univeral truth
For death is a permanent state
Seldom reckoned in our fearless youth

And the day your maker has chosen
To all who live is unknown
And never can one predict the instant
Not even the wise ones know

But the lawless 'Vagabonds' were heated, armed and
intent
On turning a peaceful gathering into
A senseless and bloody event

Weary patience in time won the day
For the path of peace in the lodges we know
Is always the better way

So remember that hearts were wounded
Remember the fragile truce
We are all mankind under heavens skies
And none should stand aloof

Sing to 'He' beyond mans gaze
Remember each morn of the Sundance days
And thank the Mounties who stood and braved
The Guns of Gustafson Lake

## The Mad Trapper
*...the story of Albert Johnson*

It was nineteen hundred and thirty one
To the northern traces the Swede had come
Albert Johnson his name lives on
Though all signs of his passage are long ago gone

The Rat River Trapper was a nasty sort
His blood boiled black from a broken heart
At the whim of a fetching femme fatale
Folks said Albert Johnson was bred in the hottest hell

The trapper came to the wastes of the north
In search of solitude and yet accursed
In the ways of the bush and the snow covered hills
The Swede was cunning and oh...ever skilled

No deadlier shot in buckskin trod
The passes and raging ravines
He bullied all who crossed his path
Like some greedy bush bound fiend

Now Constable Edgar 'Spike' Millen
Of the Royal Mounted Police
Went to find Nelson a missing man
And the bad tempered hermit Swede

He stumbled cross a dugout den
And no one answered his calls
Of a sudden lead shot tore like lightning
And made the Mountie to fall

# Tales of the High North

In hot pursuit a posse group
Set out upon the chase
O'er mountain peak
Through canyon gloom
Across the arctic wastes

The malamutes straining for each mile gaining
The Mounties pressing on
Johnson exhausted his strength long gone
Determined to make his stand

Bullets flew in a crashing din
Echoing through the land
Twenty times they hit him
But Johnson stood his stand

Then one last shot and a bullets whine
Struck him square and shattered his spine
No struggle he made nor last words to say
The demon of 'Rat River' lifeless there lay

The legends of the arctic are rife when told
And some delight in their telling
But of all the men who ventured forth
The tale of the 'Rat River' trapper accursed
Lives on in the lore of the north

## Horizon

I know there's a land where the sun sleeps at night
And the watchers watch each day
Where happiness is something to behold
And joy has no bounds in this land where 'tis told
All are kings and princes

Cheechacko gold laid at your feet
Yer malamute sated with plenty to eat
The moilers paradise

Where the mukluk shoon and unwashed crews
Dance and sing their joy
Where the veil of the northern lights
Is a shimmering beauteous gift
That lightens the desperate soul in need
And offers its priceless lift

If you've never stood and gazed o'er the tundra
On a peaceful moonlit night
And heard the silence of just one minute
A calm, eerie calm foreboding…consider this

The ice worms shrink from the distant wail
The moiler dreads the oncoming gale
For well he knows the tempest
The wolves bestirred at the blasting whirl
Of wind driven crystals a'skirl

The sky ahead is eerily dark
Where a blink before were sparkling stars
The pristine silence by maelstrom broken

# Tales of the High North

A digger caught in the oncoming rush
T'is natures rage bespoken

A howling roar of spindrift ice like needles lashing
the face
Oh father of man I beg of you please
Am I condemned to be lost without trace
The hope of relief and all of your hope
Of a battered shack barely clinging to an frozen
unstable slope

And it's just a few leagues beyond the fringe of where
no man should be
But here I am I'm lost and snared out on a frozen sea
Blind upon each compass point the needle spins and
jives
If I don't find my hovel soon I fear I'll never awaken
alive

The tales abound on the gold rush grounds
Of the spring thaw and corpses left standing
Frozen in place on the arctic wastes
Preserved in their ice coated shrouds

Soon a young sourdough joins those ghosts
A signpost of hades claim
There to await the big sleuce sweep amidst the hordes
a'driven
On the last day of days when judgment is given
And face the shining horizon arisen

## Fire on the Mountain

They gathered their kin from near and around
To strike the lode by oath all bound
And after they swore they'd buy paradise
To the devil their souls and
Gunmen their lives

They'd hoofed and rode from the eastern stands
To stake a claim in the northern lands

Along canyon sides as tall as the skies
Raging chute or damn their hides
The Chilkoot's whispering lure

From Dawson Post a boom town sprung
Where some was shot and some was hung
For there were no lawmen here at first
Where moilers came to burn their thirst
And whiskey ruled the streets

Then out of the east and over the hills
There echoed the call of a bugle shrill
Redcoated horsemen with gold striped trouse
They would decide who swung from the noose
The crown and law had arrived

The fight was fit that very night
Blood in the dirt in a show of might
The men of the Mounted gave their best
Stepping right over each hooch hounds chest
As they lay in a stooper about

# Tales of the High North

Knives did swing and chair legs too
Some took a hit from those shiny brown boots
Teeth was smashed and heads were bashed
Some timid knuckles was bruised and mashed
All in the name of the law

Fire on the mountain and hell below
A conflagration an eerie glow
The Yukon hills a'ring with the din
Civy-lization was closing in
The brigands scurried like rats

The law is here let us make it clear
Your days of sin at an end
For the Northwest Mounted have come to town
To tame the lawless and raise the crown

So cheats and thieves roll up yer sleeves
We'll settle as we must
Prepare to make a stand or bolt
The booms become a bust

Dawson's now a peaceful town and nary a shot rings
out
The Sergeant gleams with royal pride
Cuss you, you varmits hear my shout
…the towns bin culturefied

**Fate**

Have you sat neath the stars in a land afar
While the bannock baked in your pan
A gentle fire of gleaming coals
In the cut of a cedar stand

With a mangy team of malamutes
And the silence all around
Sniffed the scent of a blue norther wind
While you sat on the frozen ground

The hours passing peaceful
Though your lot is solitary
Laying whole in your buffalo robe
You ponder this sanctuary

Dreaming a dream of places unseen
Forbidden before mans eyes
You wonder amazed at heavens maze
O'er scapes beyond the skies

Gaze on the stars in awed wonderlust
Me! a speck, insignificant dust
No more than an earth bound fool

A lonely sourdough thinking of home
As you drift in the blackness of sleep
The snap of an ember, calmly you smile
…safely assured your soul is at peace

## That Grizz is Back

That Grizz is back outside my poor shack
And he'll most likely knock it down
My rusty old rifle stands idle
 I haven't a single round

Now some would just give up and run, scatter to the
hills
But this has gone on for decades now
And it's simply a battle of wills

Well here he comes he's shattered the door
We're battered and bleeding as we roll on the floor
The furniture's smashed and he'll get what he gives
Cause this time I'm gonna finish that grizz

You see that vacant place on the wall
 I'm hangin him there once he's gutted and all
When folks come to visit he's the first sight they'll
see
The natty old bear that took my leg from me

So fur's a flyin and my own hide too
But a final reckoning is overdue
I hit him a whollop with a table leg
And crashed down smashing my cottonwood bed

I bit like him and I clawed like him
And the fight continued all day
Till at last he sat upon my chest
And I thought I'd breathed my very last

Just when he went for a slashing maul
My hand found the moonshine jug
I swung it hard with the last of my strength
And it broke up side his head, now that should pain

Whiskey splashed and wasted, across the shattered
room
The bruin brewing and seething ignoring his bleeding
wound
Disgusted… he snorted, then rose and left

I lived…
Though all is askew in my broken shack
I know that old slewfoot will someday be back and…

I'm gonna git that grizz!

## The Bug Town Itch
*...a tale of the 'Tenderloin'*

Scritch and scratch up and down yer back
T'is obvious where you've been
And in this place there's only one cure
A bath and a soak in kerosene?

You've caught the mechanized lice
From the ladies of the night
And Oh! how you agonize
As they crawl and feed and bite

I've told you once and told you twice and told you
once again
In Yellowknife just cash your haul
Untie your sleigh and get away
Never yield to the lusting call

But you would not listen to the schooled and wise
And off to 'Bug Town' you went
They hooched you up
They hooked you up
You awoke with a Klondike wench

So with a foggy aching head you crawled out from
her buggy bed
All blurry eyed and sore
The stench of the brothel assailed your nostrils
As you staggered out the door

But you've brought home the gift she gave you
Have you learned?

That's the price you pay
Never return to 'Bug Town'
This time you foolish Cheechako try to heed what I
say

One more bit of advice and aside
Remember these words that I've coined
There's a damned good reason why
They call it 'The Tenderloin'

## The Bentwood Rocker

A bentwood rocker idly sits
Inside the homestead door
It's sat there now for twenty years
And never has it moved

I fear so much as touch it you see
It belonged to the woman who was mother to me
She taught me to walk
She taught me to talk
And kept me tidy and clean

She'd rock me in that rocker
And held me when I cried
She stood me hard to honesty
And caught me when I lied

Oh the pain of the mother that bore me
All in the birthing travail
A boy child held in flannel wrap
And the newborns lively wail

She loved me till the day she died twenty years ago
Words defy my longing now that I'm the one grown
old
When I get to heavens gates with sins aplenty to atone
A bentwood rocker there I'll seek among the angels
fold

## Blue Dawg is Gone

Blue Dawg is gone to the land beyond
Where the rainbows bridge from peak to peak
Spanning the cleft of valleys green
Where no dark sky or storm is seen

The buck and doe, the ermine and crow
The chipmunk and high soaring hawk
Never a word of anger or spite
Where each mans sins and wrongs are all set right

Blue Dawg dreamed of pasture scenes
While beset in the arctic freeze
He kept his faith in the Almighty
Trudging and sledding till dawn

Nary a curse or foul mouth word
Instead he prayed for salvation
Just one more day to reach his claim
In a canyon cross the tundra

The mists rolled back and there by the shack
Neath the early morning sun
His brood of Metis youngers
Danced and leapt and run

He's shaken back from his dreaming vice
Frozen solid a block of ice
The vision wasn't real
All of him that can ever remain is another wandering
soul
Only his spirit left to journey…

To the haven beyond the pole

41851351R00094

Made in the USA
San Bernardino, CA
22 November 2016